READINGS ON

A TALE OF TWO CITIES

THE GREENHAVEN PRESS
Literary Companion
TO BRITISH LITERATURE

(78)
338

READINGS ON

A TALE OF TWO CITIES

David Bender, *Publisher*
Bruno Leone, *Executive Editor*
Scott Barbour, *Managing Editor*
Bonnie Szumski, *Series Editor*
Don Nardo, *Book Editor*

Greenhaven Press, San Diego, CA

Library of Congress Cataloging-in-Publication Data

Readings on A tale of two cities / Don Nardo, book editor.
        p.   cm. — (Greenhaven Press literary companion
to British literature)
    Includes bibliographical references (p.) and index.
    ISBN 1-56510-648-2 (pbk. : alk. paper). —
ISBN 1-56510-649-0 (lib. : alk. paper)
    1. Dickens, Charles, 1719–1793.—Tale of two cities.
2. France—History—Revolution, 1789–1799—Literature
and the revolution. I. Nardo, Don, 1947–   . II. Series.
PR4571.R43   1997
823'.8—dc21   97-5019
                                                                          CIP

Cover photo: Corbis-Bettmann

Copyright ©1997 by Greenhaven Press, Inc.
PO Box 289009
San Diego, CA 92198-9009
Printed in the U.S.A.

It was the best of times, it was the worst of times, it was the age of wisdom, it was the age of foolishness, it was the epoch of belief, it was the epoch of incredulity, it was the season of Light, it was the season of Darkness, it was the spring of hope, it was the winter of despair, we had everything before us, we had nothing before us, we were all going direct to Heaven, we were all going direct the other way . . .

**Charles Dickens,
opening lines of
*A Tale of Two Cities***

CONTENTS

Chapter One: Major Themes Developed in *A Tale of Two Cities*

One of the central images in *A Tale of Two Cities*, as
in so many other works by Dickens, is the prison.
The author's mixture of fascination with and revulsion for jails derived from some vivid, painful, and
haunting childhood experiences.

A Tale of Two Cities features two very different
kinds of violence. The first, practiced by both the
upper and lower classes, is unacceptable because it
is cruel, cold, and arbitrary; the second, exemplified
by Sydney Carton's climactic sacrifice, is acceptable
because the reader perceives it as a humane and
noble act.

Rushing water that overtakes, swallows up, and
drowns its victims is a metaphor repeated frequently
throughout the pages of *A Tale of Two Cities*. And the
"vision of a drowning man" can be taken to symbolize Paris being engulfed by the relentless tide of mob
violence and the Reign of Terror.

Hangings, beheadings, and other forms of public execution constituted the ultimate exposure of a person's privacy to public view. Dickens's depictions of such executions in *A Tale of Two Cities* mirrored the way he, as all-knowing narrator, exposed his characters' private lives and thoughts.

Chapter Two: Pivotal Characters in *A Tale of Two Cities*

Dr. Manette's unjust imprisonment and ultimate release symbolize the central theme of *A Tale of Two Cities*—escape from the darkness of misery and repression into the light of love, humanity, and truth.

Chapter Three: The Treatment of Social and Historical Upheaval in *A Tale of Two Cities*

Dickens's approach to presenting the events of the French Revolution was an assault on traditional historical method, which views past events as distinct actions that lead up to and help shape the present; rather, in *A Tale of Two Cities* the present is essentially no different than the past, and the future will be little different than the present.

FOREWORD

> *"'Tis the good reader that*
> *makes the good book."*
>
> Ralph Waldo Emerson

The story's bare facts are simple: The captain, an old and scarred seafarer, walks with a peg leg made of whale ivory. He relentlessly drives his crew to hunt the world's oceans for the great white whale that crippled him. After a long search, the ship encounters the whale and a fierce battle ensues. Finally the captain drives his harpoon into the whale, but the harpoon line catches the captain about the neck and drags him to his death.

A simple story, a straightforward plot—yet, since the 1851 publication of Herman Melville's *Moby-Dick*, readers and critics have found many meanings in the struggle between Captain Ahab and the whale. To some, the novel is a cautionary tale that depicts how Ahab's obsession with revenge leads to his insanity and death. Others believe that the whale represents the unknowable secrets of the universe and that Ahab is a tragic hero who dares to challenge fate by attempting to discover this knowledge. Perhaps Melville intended Ahab as a criticism of Americans' tendency to become involved in well-intentioned but irrational causes. Or did Melville model Ahab after himself, letting his fictional character express his anger at what he perceived as a cruel and distant god?

Although literary critics disagree over the meaning of *Moby-Dick*, readers do not need to choose one particular interpretation in order to gain an understanding of Melville's novel. Instead, by examining various analyses, they can gain numerous insights into the issues that lie under the surface of the basic plot. Studying the writings of literary critics can also aid readers in making their own assessments of *Moby-Dick* and other literary works and in developing analytical thinking skills.

The Greenhaven Literary Companion Series was created with these goals in mind. Designed for young adults, this unique anthology series provides an engaging and comprehensive introduction to literary analysis and criticism. The essays included in the Literary Companion Series are chosen for their accessibility to a young adult audience and are expertly edited in consideration of both the reading and comprehension levels of this audience. In addition, each essay is introduced by a concise summation that presents the contributing writer's main themes and insights. Every anthology in the Literary Companion Series contains a varied selection of critical essays that cover a wide time span and express diverse views. Wherever possible, primary sources are represented through excerpts from authors' notebooks, letters, and journals and through contemporary criticism.

Each title in the Literary Companion Series pays careful consideration to the historical context of the particular author or literary work. In-depth biographies and detailed chronologies reveal important aspects of authors' lives and emphasize the historical events and social milieu that influenced their writings. To facilitate further research, every anthology includes primary and secondary source bibliographies of articles and/or books selected for their suitability for young adults. These engaging features make the Greenhaven Literary Companion series ideal for introducing students to literary analysis in the classroom or as a library resource for young adults researching the world's great authors and literature.

Exceptional in its focus on young adults, the Greenhaven Literary Companion Series strives to present literary criticism in a compelling and accessible format. Every title in the series is intended to spark readers' interest in leading American and world authors, to help them broaden their understanding of literature, and to encourage them to formulate their own analyses of the literary works that they read. It is the editors' hope that young adult readers will find these anthologies to be true companions in their study of literature.

INTRODUCTION

Most adults in the English-speaking world can claim to have read or studied at least one of Charles Dickens's works, for high school and college teachers in the United States and other Western nations still regularly make room in the syllabus for his novels and short stories. Many rationales have been offered for this continuing academic interest in the long-dead English author of *Oliver Twist, A Christmas Carol,* and *A Tale of Two Cities.* Most of these rationales can be conveniently gathered into two basic categories or lines of reasoning—the first historical, and the second artistic.

From the historical viewpoint, students should study Dickens because of his important position in the development of English literature. He was the first great writer to grapple with and protest loudly against the growing problems of urban civilization, including debilitating slum life, child labor, imprisonment for debt, and unsafe factory conditions. And he was something of a publishing phenomenon in his own nineteenth-century Victorian England. As literary scholar and university professor Andrew Sanders writes, Dickens was

> the quintessential artist of the new era, the Victorian writer best equipped to transform the age's restless urban civilization into art. Dickens was a best-seller at a time when the term "best-seller" did not automatically imply second-rate fiction and a sensation-craving public. . . . He is the foremost Victorian artist simply because he best reflects the complexity, the excitement, the fertility, and the often confusing abundance of contemporary England.

The particular literary qualities that helped make Dickens the quintessential and most popular writer of his age fuel the artistic rationale for studying his works today, for these qualities can be as attractive, absorbing, and entertaining to the modern reader as they were to the readers of Dickens's own time. Although the modern reader may find Dickens overly sentimental and prone to exaggeration at times, Dickens's faults are far outweighed by his strengths, not least among them his intensely vivid descriptions. Most importantly, he is a master of characterization with an uncanny facility to conjure up visual images of living, breathing persons and an incomparable command of realistic dialogue. Twentieth-century society has its own versions of these universal characters; modern readers often recognize their nineteenth-century counterparts, connect or identify with them, and thereby fall under Dickens's spell.

The essays selected for the Greenhaven Literary Companion to Charles Dickens's *A Tale of Two Cities* provide teachers and students with a wide range of information and opinion about both the novel and its author. All of the authors of the essays are or were (until their deaths) English professors at leading colleges and universities, literary scholars and critics, or scholars specializing in Dickens and his works. Many of these "Dickensians" regularly publish new books, articles, or essays exploring or debating concepts, themes, literary techniques, and characters in *A Tale of Two Cities* and other Dickens works. One of their most prestigious outlets is *Dickens Studies Annual: Essays in Victorian Fiction,* published by New York's AMS Press in cooperation with the City University of New York and Queens College, a journal from which some of the essays in this volume were taken.

This companion to Dickens's *A Tale of Two Cities* has several special features. Each of the essays explains or discusses in detail a specific, narrowly focused topic. The introduction to each essay previews the main points. And inserts interspersed within the essays exemplify ideas expressed by the authors, offer supplementary information, and/or add authenticity and color. These inserts come from Dickens's novels, from critical commentary about his works, or from other scholarly sources. Above all, this companion is designed to enhance the reader's understanding and enjoyment of one of literature's most exciting, colorful, and emotionally moving stories, a novel that, as one noted scholar puts it, beautifully captures the "flaming power" and "conveys the tumultuous sweep" of the violent French Revolution.

THE PROMISE OF A BETTER FUTURE: DICKENS AND *A TALE OF TWO CITIES*

The scene is a scaffold in Paris during the French Revolution. A large crowd of spectators has gathered to watch the brutal beheading of a group of condemned prisoners, most of them French aristocrats or persons condemned as sympathizers or accomplices of the nobility. In one of the carts heading for the scaffold stands a man holding a young girl's hand. "Down Evrémonde!" comes a cry from the bloodthirsty crowd. "To the Guillotine all aristocrats! Down Evrémonde!"

But unbeknownst to the crowd, the man in the cart is not Charles Darnay, relative of the now dead but still much hated Marquis St. Evrémonde, who frequently mistreated servants and other commoners. The prisoner heading to his death is instead Sydney Carton, an English lawyer. The night before, Carton, out of his own love and respect for Darnay's wife, Lucie, helped Darnay escape prison and now faces the dreaded blade in his place. Having wasted his life in idleness and drink, Carton finally feels that he is doing something good and worthy. Even as he stands near the steps of the scaffold, he continues to comfort the young girl, a seamstress.

"But for you, dear stranger, I should not be so composed," she tells him. "I think you were sent to me by Heaven."

"Or you to me," says Carton. "Keep your eyes upon me, dear child, and mind no other object." Seconds later, the crowd shouts its approval as she is executed; and then Sydney Carton himself begins his fateful ascent of the scaffold steps.

For most readers, this final scene of the novel *A Tale of Two Cities* is one of the most moving passages in all of literature. It must have been just as moving to write, for its author, Charles Dickens, closely identified with both Carton and Darnay, who in looks are nearly twins but whose characters are seemingly very different. In Dickens's mind, the two men—one worthy, the other unworthy—represent opposing sides of the human coin that is himself. As Dickens biographer Fred Kaplan puts it,

> They become one figure, two parts of Dickens' personality that are united in art, though it is Carton whose energy and imagination most resemble his. Between the two characters, he creates ... [a] self-portrait that, while it emphasizes the ... potential for self-destruction, unites opposites into an idealized version of love. ... Though Carton dies, he lives in Lucie, Darnay, and their daughter. At the end, Darnay is an idealized version of Carton transformed and Dickens fulfilled.

According to this view, Dickens was plagued by self-doubt about his own worth, both as an artist and a person, and used Carton's sacrifice as a way of working out his feelings. Put another way, Dickens seems to be saying that within every person, no matter how unworthy he or she might seem, dwells an element of goodness waiting for its chance to prove itself.

THE UPS AND DOWNS OF CHARLES DICKENS'S YOUTH

The man who used the themes of self-sacrifice and personal redemption to create grand drama in *A Tale of Two Cities* was born on February 7, 1812, in Landport, a section of Portsea (itself part of the greater city of Portsmouth), England, about seventy miles southwest of London. He was christened Charles John Huffham Dickens. His parents, John and Elizabeth Dickens, had seven other children, two of whom died in childhood; of those who survived, only one, Charles's sister Fanny, was older than he.

John Dickens worked as a clerk in the British Navy Pay Office at Portsea. His pay was modest and he and his wife were poor money managers, with the result that they were almost constantly in debt. Because of their inability to pay their bills, often including their rent, they were frequently compelled to move, usually to successively poorer lodgings. The navy also regularly reassigned the elder Dickens, necessitating more moves for the family, which eventually ended up in London. This combination of physical and financial instability took its toll on the children, including Charles, who only rarely benefited from any formal schooling. Nevertheless, his mother taught him to read and before the age of ten he often escaped from his insecure and sometimes unhappy home life by roaming through the imaginary worlds of books like Cervantes's *Don Quixote*, Defoe's *Robinson Crusoe*, and *The Arabian Nights*.

The family's financial downward spiral and the emotional anxieties that attended it reached their lowest ebb early in 1824. To help make ends meet, the Dickenses arranged for twelve-year-old Charles to work in a shoe-polish factory, Warren's Blacking, in a section of London called the Strand. In dingy, filthy, rat-infested surroundings, the boy had to endure long hours each day at the monotonous task of attaching labels to pots of shoe blacking. Most of his companions were lower class, illiterate, and ignorant and Charles, who dreamed of someday becoming a scholar, felt both humiliated and abandoned by his parents. It was a psychological wound that would never heal. He later wrote in his autobiography:

> No words can express the secret agony of my soul as I sunk into this companionship; compared these everyday associates with those of my happier childhood; and felt my early hopes of growing up to be a learned and distinguished man, crushed in my breast. . . . My whole nature was so penetrated with the grief and humiliation of such considerations, that even now, famous . . . and happy, I often forget in my dreams that I have a dear wife and children; even that I am a man; and wander desolately back to that time of my life.

Making matters worse, less than a month after Charles began working at the factory, his father was arrested for failure to pay a debt. At the time, English law allowed a person to press charges against another for defaulting on a loan, and many debtors languished and even died in prison. In late February 1824, John Dickens was incarcerated in London's Marshalsea prison and his appeals to relatives and friends for the money needed for his release were unsuccessful. Unable to support herself and the children on her own, Elizabeth Dickens was forced to sell most of the family's possessions and then move, along with some of the children, into the prison cell with her husband.

Still employed at Warren's Blacking, Charles lodged with a kindly family friend, Elizabeth Roylance. But in his few free hours, mostly in the evenings, the lonely, underfed boy visited his family in the prison. The misery and degradation of prison life made a deeply powerful impression on him, so powerful that images of jails and the idea of imprisonment later became important recurring themes in his works. From Fleet Prison in *The Pickwick Papers* to the debtor's prison in *Bleak House*, to the workhouse in *Oliver Twist*, to the dreaded Bastille in *A Tale of Two Cities*, Dickens used prison as a symbol of despair, injustice, and inhumane treatment. At the same time, Dickens's fascination with and revulsion for imprisonment and injustice were intensified by what he viewed as his own servitude in the shoe polish factory. As literary scholar Edgar Johnson remarks:

> All the rest of his life he lay under those two shadows—the shadow of the Marshalsea and the imprisoning shades of that dungeon workroom in which he had toiled day after despairing day. The experience opened the floodgates of his sympathy for all victims of injustice, all the neglected and misused, the innocent and suffering of the world. Their cause became his, because in the depths of his being they and he were one.

BETTER TIMES AND EARLY SUCCESSES

Luckily for young Charles Dickens and his beleaguered parents and siblings, their miserable situation soon began to improve. In late May 1824, John Dickens was released from prison under the Insolvent Debtor's Act, a bankruptcy provision that granted freedom to those who filed for release, but left them penniless and humiliated; and not long afterward he received a small inheritance from a deceased relative, enabling him to support his family once more, however modestly. In the early summer of that year Charles left the factory and finally began attending a formal school—Wellington House Academy, on Hampstead Road in London. But the boy's education was relatively brief. Feeling the pinch of the family's continued financial straits, in May 1827 Elizabeth Dickens took her son out of the Wellington school and found him a position as a low-level clerk in the office of a lawyer named Edward Blackmore.

Dickens's experience in the law office was a springboard to bigger and better things. He worked hard and learned as much as possible about the law; and all the while he acquired skills and interests that would become useful later. He learned shorthand, for example, which allowed him to become a court reporter while still in his teens, and he also became an avid theater buff, spending much of his free time organizing amateur play productions. His skill, ambition, and energy were impressive enough to get him admitted as a reporter to the British House of Commons (somewhat equivalent to the U.S. House of Representatives) in 1831, when he was only nineteen. He also hired out as a reporter for various well-known newspapers, including the *True Sun, Mirror of Parliament,* and *Morning Chronicle.*

During this period Dickens first tried his hand at writing fiction. He managed to publish some stories, for which he received no money, in the *Old Monthly Magazine*. Then, when the *Morning Chronicle* circulated an evening edition, he began contributing short comic "sketches" for pay under the pen name of "Boz." A collection of these pieces appeared in book form under the title *Sketches by Boz*, the popularity of which was boosted by its beautiful and charming illustrations, supplied by the prominent artist George Cruikshank. While turning out the Boz sketches, Dickens worked closely with the manager of the new *Evening Chronicle*, George Hogarth, and soon began courting one of Hogarth's three daughters, Catherine. On April 2, 1836, Charles and Catherine were married.

The marriage seemed to signal the start of a happy and fruitful period for Dickens, for the ceremony took place just two days after he published the opening installment of his first important and successful work, *The Pickwick Papers*. Like so many of his works to come, including the immortal *A Tale of Two Cities*, *Pickwick* first appeared in monthly magazine installments and came out in book form later. By the end of its serialization in 1837, *Pickwick* was immensely popular and hugely profitable. From that time on, Charles Dickens was the most popular English novelist in his own lifetime and, arguably, has been ever since. Other fortunate events followed between 1837 and 1839, including the birth of the Dickenses' first three children, Mary, Kate, and Walter (they had ten children in all), and the beginning of Charles's friendship with journalist John Forster, who would eventually become his first biographer.

This two-year period also saw the serialization of Dickens's second novel, *Oliver Twist*, the story of the adventures of a poor foundling (a child abandoned by unknown parents) and his life among London's thieves and other streetwise characters. As scholar Walter Allen comments, the mood and content of *Oliver Twist* were quite different from those of *The Pickwick Papers:*

> The two novels show the two sides of Dickens' genius. *Pickwick* is a work of pure humor, in which the crudities and miseries of the real world are sterilized by laughter and the vicious are objects of comedy. . . . The world of *Pickwick* is almost fairyland. In *Oliver Twist*, fairyland has become the country of nightmare; the bar fairies have become ogres. There is still laughter, but it has become savage, satirical. . . .

On the surface, *Oliver Twist* is an exposure novel, an attack on the working of the poor law of the day, but its real theme is the fate of innocence and weakness.... From then on, fairyland and nightmare exist side by side in Dickens' novels.

DICKENS AS SOCIAL REFORMER

Indeed, in work after work Dickens skillfully combined moments of charm, grace, and humor with gripping descriptions of poverty, snobbery and strife within and between classes, and other social ills of his time. And the author became so popular that his exposés of such ills were sometimes instrumental in helping to alleviate them. *Nicholas Nickleby*, for instance, which followed *Oliver Twist* in the late 1830s, was in part a concerted attack on those English schools, then quite common, in which cruel headmasters brutally beat and often half-starved their students. The public reaction to Dickens's vivid descriptions of abuse was immediate and extreme: Thousands of parents withdrew their children from such schools, which then were forced to close their doors. Such closings were so widespread, in fact, that in 1864 a school commissioner reported, "I have wholly failed to discover an example of the typical Yorkshire school with which Dickens has made us familiar."

Similar criticisms and attacks on social ills appeared even in Dickens's shorter and ostensibly lighter works. A perfect example is the classic *A Christmas Carol* (variously defined as a long short story or short novel), first published in 1843. On one level the colorful and charming tale of the transformation of the mean, penny-pinching Mr. Scrooge by the three ghosts of Christmas, the work touches on three of Dickens's favorite recurring themes—the prison, the plight of the poor masses, and the insensitivity of the upper classes to this plight. The following scene, in which two men ask Scrooge to contribute to charity, strongly foreshadows the more complex development of these same themes in *A Tale of Two Cities:*

> "At this festive season of the year, Mr. Scrooge," said the gentleman, taking up his pen, "it is more than usually desirable that we should make some slight provision for the poor and destitute, who suffer greatly at the present time. Many thousands are in want of common necessaries; hundreds of thousands are in want of common comforts, sir."
>
> "Are there no prisons?" asked Scrooge.
>
> "Plenty of prisons," said the gentleman, laying down his

pen again.

"And the union workhouses?" demanded Scrooge. "Are they still in operation?"

"They are.". . .

"I wish to be left alone," said Scrooge. . . . "I help to support the establishments I have mentioned—they cost enough; and those who are badly off must go there."

"Many can't go there; and many would rather die."

"If they would rather die," said Scrooge, "they had better do it, and decrease the surplus population."

At the time *A Christmas Carol* appeared, Dickens was already a wealthy man. He built a large house for his immediate family, as well as a smaller one in the countryside for his parents, and maintained a very comfortable lifestyle thereafter. The bitter memories of his childhood poverty and humiliation remained sources of shame and emotional pain, however, and he periodically lost his temper with his parents, whom he held partially responsible.

Dickens nevertheless loved his parents and used them as models for various characters in his books. The colorful Mr. Micawber in *David Copperfield,* for example, was based in large degree on John Dickens. And both Mrs. Nickleby in *Nicholas Nickleby* and the strange, reclusive Miss Havisham in *Great Expectations* were patterned substantially after Elizabeth Dickens (in the latter case when she had turned senile shortly before her death in 1863).

DICKENS'S CREATIONS

Mr. Scrooge, Mr. Micawber, and Miss Havisham are but three of the hundreds of memorable characters Dickens created in his books and stories during a prosperous, thirty-year career. In fact, broadly drawn yet highly realistic characters—some delightfully quaint, some shifty or slimy, others bumbling and comic—became one of the author's trademarks. "There are creations of Mr. Dickens," wrote English novelist and satirist William Makepeace Thackeray in 1852, "figures so delightful, that one feels happier and better for knowing them, as one does for being brought into the society of very good men and women."

Among this remarkable gallery of literary personages was, for example, the sublimely comic Mrs. Gamp in the novel *Martin Chuzzlewit,* serialized in 1843–1844, shortly after Dickens returned from a tour of the United States. Dickens had been excited and optimistic about the visit beforehand, but his firsthand views of American slavery and the crudeness of American cultural pursuits, as compared with those in Europe, soured him; *Martin Chuzzlewit* is filled with unflattering caricatures of obnoxious American types. Other well-drawn and memorable Dickensian characters are Serjeant Buzfuz and Alfred Jingle in *The Pickwick Papers* (1837), Mr. Brass and Mr. Quilp in *The Old Curiosity Shop* (1840), Mr. Tappertit and Miss Miggs in *Barnaby Rudge* (1841), Uriah Heep in *David Copperfield* (1849), Harold Skimpole in *Bleak House* (1852), and Pip and Abel Magwitch in *Great Expectations* (1860).

Dickens created two of his greatest characters—Sydney Carton and Madame Defarge—for *A Tale of Two Cities*. But in this Dickens novel, unlike so many others, characterization took a backseat to plot and the epic sweep of the events the story described. These were the dramatic and bloody events of the French Revolution, which began in 1789, twenty-three years before Dickens was born. He had apparently been fascinated by the Revolution throughout his adult life but did not set himself to a fictional treatment of it until 1859. In that year he established the weekly literary magazine *All the Year Round* (he had for years been the editor of the journal *Household Words*), and the novel appeared in that publication in installment form between April 20 and November 26. The book version was released in December.

By this time, Dickens's private life was no longer as placid and happy as it had been during the first several years of his marriage. His wife, convinced that he was having an affair with an actress named Ellen Ternan (a charge that may or may not have been true; in any case, he *had* fallen in love with Ternan), pushed for a legal separation, which occurred in 1858, shortly before he began researching *A Tale of Two Cities*. His usual composure shaken, Dickens had thrown himself into his work with a vengeance, not only continuing with his writing, editing, and involvement in amateur theater productions, but also giving public readings of his works and lobbying politicians and others for social reforms (over the years, he periodically backed such causes as the establishment of a home for reformed prostitutes and the clearing or renovation of slum housing).

These and other often strenuous and/or stressful activities continued after the completion of *Tale*, and overwork steadily began impairing Dickens's health. In the late 1860s, he again toured the United States, this time for a series of readings. His opinion of Americans had improved somewhat, as evidenced by his description of one of his New York audiences: "They are a wonderfully fine audience, even better than Edinburgh [Scotland], and almost, if not quite as good as Paris." But though the tour was an unqualified success, the strain exhausted his already frail constitution. He grew steadily weaker and died on June 9, 1870, while working on a new novel, *The Mystery of Edwin Drood.* He was buried in Westminster Abbey in London beside Chaucer and other English literary greats. One of the best and most touching tributes to Dickens's talent and contributions was given by the American writer Kate Douglas Wiggin (author of *Rebecca of Sunnybrook Farm*) in her 1912 work, *A Child's Journey with Dickens:*

> He had his literary weaknesses, Charles Dickens, but they were all dear, big attractive ones, virtues grown a bit wild and rank. Somehow when you put him—with his elemental humor, his inexhaustible vitality, his humanity, sympathy and pity—beside the Impeccables [those authors deemed more perfect craftsmen], he always looms large! Just for a moment, when the heart overpowers the reason, he even makes the flawless ones look a little faded and colorless.

ANYTHING BUT TYPICAL

To be sure, *A Tale of Two Cities* possesses all the qualities Wiggin cites as being typical of a Dickens novel—vitality, color, humanity, and pity—all in abundance. Indeed, the story is filled with the same kind of picturesque, quirky characters, highly atmospheric scenes, and deeply sympathetic treatment of the plight of the downtrodden that one normally associates with Dickens. Yet *Tale* is anything but a typical Dickens novel. One factor that sets it apart is that it is one of only two historical novels he wrote, the other being *Barnaby Rudge*, about England's anti-Catholic Gordon Riots of 1780.

The basic premise for the story of *Tale* came from *The Frozen Deep*, a play by Dickens's longtime theatrical friend, Wilkie Collins. Dickens had produced the play for the stage in 1857 and had himself played the role of a man, one of two who love the same woman, who gives his life to save that of his rival. Dickens openly acknowledges his debt to Collins's play in the first sentence of the novel's preface:

> When I was acting, with my children and friends, in Mr. Wilkie Collins' drama of *The Frozen Deep*, I first conceived the

main idea of the story. A strong desire was upon me then, to embody it in my own person; and I traced out in my fancy, the state of mind of which it would necessitate the presentation to an observant spectator, with particular care and interest.

The preface to *Tale* also acknowledges Dickens's debt to another friend, the great Scottish historian Thomas Carlyle. "No one can hope to add anything to the philosophy of Mr. Carlyle's wonderful book," he writes, in reference to Carlyle's massive 1837 volume, *A History of the French Revolution,* which was already considered a classic of its kind. The book became an essential reference for Dickens in his attempts to construct a realistic and authentic historical background for his fictional characters and their exploits. In fact, Carlyle provided almost all of the primary source material for Dickens's research for the novel. When the novelist asked his friend to provide him with a few extra reference books about the Revolution, Carlyle sent him two large cartloads of volumes, many from his own impressive collection. Dickens endeavored to at least skim them all and so immersed himself in the subject that he read nothing else in the many months it took him to write *Tale.* One must not suppose, however, that Dickens simply reproduced Carlyle's style and philosophical views of the Revolution. As scholar of English literature Henry Hubert explains:

> Dickens and Carlyle were quite different types: Carlyle, a noted scholar, collecting and sifting many documents to produce his great work; Dickens, a badly educated man who gathered his material through carefully observing the people and events about him. It was Dickens' genius that he could write about a city and an event about which he knew next to nothing and produce such a stirring, believable portrait of the time. . . . Carlyle, as he writes, stands aloof from the whirlpool, and one feels that if he had lived at the time he would have protested against the abuses [of the French peasants by the nobility] and left it at that. Whereas we have the feeling as we read *A Tale of Two Cities* that Dickens, a man who believed passionately in eradicating any social injustice he came upon, would have joined the mob and stormed the Bastille.

Another factor that makes *Tale* different from most of Dickens's other novels is that the work is driven by its plot rather than its characters. Novels such as *David Copperfield* and *Great Expectations* are full of well-drawn characters who become involved in numerous, and sometimes unrelated, incidents and interactions. The story lines are generally defined by these interactions and often seem to ramble along in an episodic fashion, so that the reader has no clear idea of what will happen next. By contrast, *Tale* has far fewer characters. And instead of being the main focus of the story, the principal characters are, in a sense, pawns carried along in the irresistible tide of the story's larger events. Because these events actually happened, to that extent the narrative is preordained and inevitable; historical events, therefore, determine in large degree the characters' actions.

STRESS, STRAIN, AND DARK MOODS

Still another factor that makes *A Tale of Two Cities* an atypical Dickens novel is that it is shorter than most, only about 100,000 words, compared with more usual lengths of some 380,000 words. This is partly because he was attempting for the first time the very difficult task of serializing the book in both weekly and monthly versions of *All the Year Round.* Working on weekly and monthly installments at the same time forced him to condense his material more than he usually did, which proved frustrating and stressful. In August 1859, he wrote to John Forster, "Nothing but the interest of the subject, and the pleasure of striving with the difficulty of the forms of the treatment, nothing in the mere way of money, I mean, could also repay the time and trouble of the incessant condensation."

Other factors troubled Dickens while he was working on *Tale.* Among them were the strain of meeting so many deadlines, the extreme seriousness of the subject matter, the fact that he personally identified so strongly with the dissipated main character, Sydney Carton, and the stress brought on by his recent separation from his wife. All of these combined to make the writing of *Tale* an unusually difficult and emotional experience for Dickens. "Throughout its execution," he said in the latter stages of the task, "it has had complete possession of me; I have so far verified what it has done and suffered it all myself." At one point, he told Forster that certain aspects of the work "drive me frantic."

Dickens's dark moods while writing the novel were likely partly motivated by and certainly reflected in the work's dark and serious themes. Noted modern Dickens biographer Peter Ackroyd points out that the story is

> filled with images of horror and destruction, of dirt and disease, of imprisonment and violent death. The central image is one of resurrection, but this encompasses the stealing of

dead bodies from their graves as well as the more spiritual resurrection which Sydney Carton so much longs for. This is a world of enormous shadows, of the setting sun, of night; the only illumination occurs in the glare of the French Revolution itself, as if the only alternative to the darkness of despair lies in the rage and destructiveness of that event.

No less morbid is Dickens's frequent use of symbols to suggest and reinforce images of death and bloodletting. In a striking example that appears early in the story, a wine cask shatters and spills its contents into a gutter. Dozens of people converge to lap up the wine and their feet, shoes, and mouths become stained with red, foreshadowing what will become real wounds in the frightening bloodbath of the Revolution to come. The only major incident in the novel that lifts the reader out of this seemingly relentless onslaught of gloom and doom is Sydney Carton's sacrifice, which allows Lucie and her family to escape, and at the same time redeems Carton from his own wasted life.

Literary Objections to the Novel

Indeed, it is the almost unrelenting seriousness of *Tale*'s themes and tone that has prompted much of the literary criticism leveled at it over the years. One of the strongest objections to the novel's lack of humor comes from the noted scholar and Dickens authority George Gissing, who writes, "*A Tale of Two Cities* is not characteristic of Dickens in anything but theme (the attack on social tyranny). With humor lacking we feel the restraint throughout." Gissing added that the novel "leaves no strong impression on the mind; even the figure of Carton grows dim against a dimmer background." Countering this argument, Henry Hubert speaks for many other scholars who find no fault with the book's serious tone. "True," he says,

> humor is an obvious component of most of Dickens' other novels and many of Dickens' greatest creations are comic characters. It does not necessarily follow, however, that therefore there should be some great comic characters in *A Tale of Two Cities*. Strong humor would be out of place in this story. . . . Ironically, those people who have not read Dickens enjoy *A Tale of Two Cities* most, while ardent Dickens advocates are disappointed with it . . . largely because of the missing element of humor.

Another common scholarly criticism of *Tale* is that it lapses too often into sentimentality; that is, that the author overdoes certain passages of description and dialogue in a manipulative attempt to stir his readers' emotions. The scene in which Lucie first sees her father after his release from the prison and the stirring moments preceding Carton's death on the scaffold are often singled out as being too "weepy." And still another frequently raised objection to the novel is Dickens's use, or in the critics' view overuse, of the device of coincidence. Edgar Johnson sums up his objection:

> It is too neat that the wineshop-keeper Defarge should be Dr. Manette's old servant and that Madame Defarge should be a younger sister of that wronged pair whose deaths the Doctor had witnessed. It is somewhat forced that Darnay, the innocent scion [descendant] of the wicked St. Evrémonde family, should not only become the Doctor's son-in-law but should be drawn to Paris.... On top of these coincidences, John Basard, the prison spy and turnkey, turns out to be Miss Pross's brother, and Jerry Cruncher is opportunely at hand to provide Sydney Carton with a damaging piece of knowledge against him. Finally—the supreme coincidence of all—Carton resembles Darnay so closely as to be able without detection to substitute for him. Cleverly though Dickens prepares for these implausibilities, even his consummate ingenuity leaves it unconvincing that there should be so many of them.

Yet such objections to some of the literary devices Dickens employs in the novel ultimately appear minor when the work is viewed as a whole. In spite of continued differences of opinion about the overuse of sentiment and coincidence and other supposed shortcomings of the work, no critic denies the overall power of the story's narrative, its epic sweep and color, its often gripping human situations and dilemmas, and the compelling dramatization of Carton's final transformation and redemption. Who, on reading the climactic scene, has not imagined him- or herself in the same harrowing situation and wondered if he or she would act as unselfishly, bravely, and nobly as Carton does?

In fact, it is the dramatic, heartrending, and compelling nature of this final scene that afforded Dickens the chance to make the most important and sublime statement of the book, perhaps one of the greatest of all his books; for he was well aware that most readers would, like himself, identify with, or at least stand in awe of, Carton and his sacrifice. Dickens realized that everyone would see this act, regardless of whether they believed it foolhardy or thought they would or could do it themselves, as the ultimately good and right thing to do.

Recall the stirring lines provided by the narrator after

Carton has met his end; Dickens brilliantly presents these as a kind of "stream of consciousness," as if they might have been the doomed man's last thoughts as he climbs the scaffold steps and places his head beneath the blade. These last thoughts are exalted ones, as Carton looks beyond his own death and the horrors of the Revolution to a brighter, better future: "I see a beautiful city and a brilliant people rising from this abyss." He goes on to propose that the evils that spawned the Revolution, as well as the terrors perpetrated in the rebellion itself, will eventually fade in importance and give way to kinder, saner conditions.

Then he turns his mind's eye to Lucie and her family. "I see the lives for which I lay down my life, peaceful, useful, prosperous and happy, in that England which I shall see no more. I see her with a child upon her bosom, who bears my name." Carton's thoughts suddenly leap ahead and he sees Lucie as an old woman, weeping on the anniversary of this, his final day; still she honors his brave sacrifice, which allowed her to live a happy and fulfilled life with those she loved. He also sees the child Lucie named after him, now grown and becoming the success in life that he himself was not:

> I see him, foremost of just judges and honoured men, bringing a boy of my name, with a forehead that I know and golden hair, to this place—then fair to look upon, with not a trace of this day's disfigurement—and I hear him tell the child my story, with a tender and a faltering voice.

> It is a far, far better thing that I do, than I have ever done; it is a far, far better rest that I go to, than I have ever known.

With these magnificent concluding lines, Dickens leads the reader out of the depths of misery, rebellion, social chaos, bloodshed, and hopelessness and onto a higher plane of love, hope, and human triumph. And Carton's noble act stands as a shining example for everyone who has ever loved. Indeed, in this scene Dickens seems to say that the qualities of goodness and selflessness that Carton displays in his last moments exist in all of us, latent, beneath the surface, waiting for their best and most appropriate moment of expression. In this way, Charles Dickens expresses his optimistic belief that, despite the ravages of ignorance, neglect, cruelty, injustice, and all the other ills he raged against throughout his career, humanity harbors the potential to fulfill the promise of a better future.

CHAPTER 1

Major Themes Developed in *A Tale of Two Cities*

READINGS ON
A TALE OF TWO CITIES

Dickens's Use of the Motif of Imprisonment

Edgar Johnson

In the following article, former English professor at the City College of New York and noted Dickens scholar Edgar Johnson offers an insightful examination of how Dickens employed a thematic motif that haunted the novelist throughout his life—that of imprisonment. Johnson points out images of the jail that appear repeatedly in Dickens's novels and stories and are especially prominent in *A Tale of Two Cities*. Johnson takes this theme one step further, contending that Dickens seemed almost obsessed with the idea that people, including himself, could be, in a very real sense, imprisoned in unhappy marriages, relationships, and professions. Thus, the imprisonment scenes in *Tale*, suggests Johnson, reflect the author's own feelings of entrapment in a failed marriage.

A Tale of Two Cities is both the least typical of all Dickens' novels and the one that most deeply symbolizes the entire drive of his career.... It has none of the discursive elaboration of episode and character that makes his more monumental novels resemble some intricate Gothic cathedral, bursting out into casual substructures and comic detail and crowded with incidental figures. The Vincent Crummles theatrical troupe, for example, in *Nicholas Nickleby*, are pure frisky embroidery; Quilp, the malign dwarf of *The Old Curiosity Shop*, is a demon from a frieze; little Miss Mowcher and Uriah Heep in *David Copperfield* are gargoyles; and the oily Chadband, in *Bleak House*, might have provided some medieval carver with the model for a fat monk squatting cross-legged on the capital of a column.

In contrast, the plot of *A Tale of Two Cities* subdues every detail to its stark speed of purpose. All of its small group of characters are essential to their function, none introduced merely for fun or in sheer creative ecstasy.... With only the smallest glints of comedic exception, *A Tale of Two Cities* concentrates fierily upon the blood-bathed violence of the French Revolution and the Reign of Terror which are both its setting and its theme.... [Dickens's] whole development ... almost irresistibly led him to portray the violent rebellion of an entire people sweeping away the foundations of a rotten and corrupt system. Once before, in *Barnaby Rudge*, he had depicted an outburst of mob fury, the Gordon Riots of 1780, but tumultuously as Dickens there rendered the storming of Newgate [Prison], the surrender of that prison was the alarm bell of no such national cataclysm as the fall of the Bastille. *A Tale of Two Cities* rises stormily to its greater theme in a wild turmoil of lurid power and sympathetic understanding.

THE IMAGE OF THE JAIL

If its theme is thus central to Dickens' work, its key image is central to his interpretation of that theme. That image is the jail. Dr. Manette has been driven mad, broken and goaded into a destroying curse, by eighteen years' unjust imprisonment in the Bastille. When we first meet Charles Darnay, he is a prisoner in Newgate charged with being a traitor and spy. In the great circle of the narrative's movement, Darnay is again imprisoned, this time in the Conciergerie, a victim of his family's past deeds of exploitation and cruelty, and is saved from death only by the sacrifice of Sydney Carton, who takes his place beneath the blade of the guillotine. These dominant scenes of incarceration are archetypal symbols in the book. The long imprisonment of Dr. Manette is representative of the fate of the entire French people, immured within the walls of an unyielding social system. The destruction of the Bastille is both a literal and a symbolic statement of rebellion smashing those prison walls.

It is striking to note the constant recurrence of the jail image in Dickens' work. The Fleet Prison in *Pickwick*, the King's Bench Prison in *Nicholas Nickleby* and again in *David Copperfield*, Newgate in *Barnaby Rudge*, both the Marseilles jail and the Marshalsea in *Little Dorrit*, the prison hulks from which Magwitch escapes in *Great Expectations* and the jail in which he dies, the barred cell from which, in *Oliver Twist*,

Fagin is dragged to be hanged, the debtors' prison in *Bleak House* within which Gridley dies and which Richard Carstone escapes only by dying of despair, the condemned cell waiting for the murderer in *Edwin Drood*—jails are omnipresent in the novels from first to last. But, more than that, the orphanage and the workhouse in *Oliver Twist* and *Our Mutual Friend* are bleak places of confinement analogous to jails, a fact underlined by their being known to the nineteenth-century poor as "bastilles." Both the factory and the school-room in *Hard Times* are jail-like; in *Our Mutual Friend* all London is described as a gloomy and enormous jail. Miss Havisham in *Great Expectations* is self-incarcerated in her dark, decaying house; for the lawyer, Mr. Jaggers, and Wemmick, his clerk, their office in Little Britain is a kind of dungeon within which they lock away their better selves; and Pip's desperate and disillusioned infatuation with Estella is the darkest emotional captivity of all. *Little Dorrit* culminatingly sees all of human existence, for rich and poor, for the imprisoned and the free, as no more than confinement in a variety of jails.

LIVING UNDER TWO SHADOWS

So compulsive a recurrence of jails and prison imagery can only be deeply rooted in emotional experience. Such is indeed the fact. The scenes of David Copperfield's despairing enslavement in Murdstone and Grinby's bottling warehouse and of Mr. Micawber's confinement in the King's Bench Prison give some hint of what that experience had been. For when Dickens was twelve his father had been imprisoned in the Marshalsea for debt and the child had been obliged to give up school and sink into a menial job wrapping bottles in Jonathan Warren's blacking warehouse in Hungerford Stairs [in the district known as the Strand]. A sensitive and extraordinarily ambitious child, he was plunged by the catastrophe into bewildered and hopeless misery. . . .

The wound was so deep that its psychological scars were never eradicated. Dickens could never bear to tell his wife and children either of his father's confinement in the Marshalsea or of his own imprisonment in the blacking warehouse. For years he could not endure going near Hungerford Stairs; for years when, walking in the Strand, he drew near another blacking establishment, he crossed the street to avoid smelling the cement of the blacking corks. . . .

WHAT MR. PICKWICK SAW IN THE PRISON CELLS

The following excerpt from The Pickwick Papers, *in which Mr. Pickwick surveys his surroundings after arriving in Fleet Prison, is typical of Dickens's frequent use of jail imagery.*

It was getting dark; that is to say, a few gas jets were kindled in this place which was never light, by way of compliment to the evening, which had set in outside. As it was rather warm, some of the tenants of the numerous little rooms which opened into the gallery on either hand, had set their doors ajar. Mr Pickwick peeped into them as he passed along, with great curiosity and interest. Here four or five great hulking fellows, just visible through a cloud of tobacco-smoke, were engaged in noisy and riotous conversation over half-emptied pots of beer, or playing at all-fours with a very greasy pack of cards. In the adjoining room, some solitary tenant might be seen, poring, by the light of a feeble tallow candle, over a bundle of soiled and tattered papers, yellow with dust and dropping to pieces from age: writing for the hundredth time, some lengthened statement of his grievances, for the perusal of some great man whose eyes it would never reach, or whose heart it would never touch. In a third, a man, with his wife and a whole crowd of children, might be seen making up a scanty bed on the ground, or upon a few chairs, for the younger ones to pass the night in. And in a fourth, and a fifth, and a sixth, and a seventh, the noise, and the beer, and the tobacco-smoke, and the cards, all came over again in greater force than before. . . .

There were many classes of people here, from the labouring man in his fustian jacket, to the broken-down spendthrift in his shawl dressing-gown, most appropriately out at elbows; but there was the same air about them all—a listless jail-bird careless swagger, a vagabondish who's-afraid sort of bearing, which is wholly indescribable in words, but which any man can understand in one moment if he wish, by setting foot in the nearest debtor's prison, and looking at the very first group of people he sees there, with the same interest as Mr Pickwick did.

It is plain that the blacking warehouse was for Dickens no less a place of imprisonment than the Marshalsea which had swallowed his father at the same time. All the rest of his life he lay under those two shadows—the shadow of the Marshalsea and the imprisoning shades of that dungeon workroom in which he had toiled day after despairing day. The experience opened the floodgates of his sympathy for all victims of injustice, all the neglected and misused, the innocent and suffering of the world. Their cause became his, because in the depths of his being they and he were one. Even when they rebelled with maddened ferocity, and fell into excesses of destruction and cruelty, a strange flame of exultation burned amid his horror as he revealed the hell fury that oppression can kindle to molten intensity in poor men's hearts.

WEIGHED DOWN WITH CHAINS

But *A Tale of Two Cities* had additional roots in frustrations more recent but no less vehement than the humiliations of Dickens' childhood. His once-happy marriage with Catherine Hogarth had by slow degrees grown more and more unhappy for them both. They were no longer companions; like poor David Copperfield in his marriage with his child-wife, Dickens had discovered that his marriage was the "mistaken impulse of an undisciplined heart," and that he and Catherine made each other miserable. For the sake of their children he had tried to make the best of it and stifle his unhappiness within his breast, but this too came to seem still another form of imprisonment.

Then, in 1857, while he was acting in a benefit production of his friend Wilkie Collins' melodrama *The Frozen Deep*, he fell in love with Ellen Ternan, a young actress in the cast. Dickens' role in the play was that of Richard Wardour, a member of a polar expedition who saves from death his rival in love at the cost of his own life, and dies in the arms of his beloved, with her tears raining down upon his face. During every night's performance Dickens tore himself to pieces under the eyes of the fair and unattainable creature whom his imprisoning marriage rendered hopelessly remote, whom it rent and tortured his spirit to give up, but who seemed as inaccessible as the blue sky of freedom to a wretched captive in a jail. During the months that followed, Dickens thought of his marriage as an iron-barred and stone-walled misery weighed down with adamantine chains from which he could never escape.

Then, suddenly, in the following spring, Catherine learned of his infatuation. Although Dickens insisted that he had not been unfaithful to her, she refused to believe him and, goaded on by her family, pressed for the separation that he had considered hopeless. Even so, Dickens had not desired an open break or the scandal of a public separation which was now forced upon him. But by the summer of 1858 agreements had been made and Dickens and his wife went their separate ways.

RECALLED TO LIFE

It was out of all these emotional sources, both those deeply rooted in the past and the anguish of these more recent nights and days, that *A Tale of Two Cities* was born. The idea for the story had come to him while he was acting Richard Wardour; and Sydney Carton's sacrifice of his life amid the flames of revolution magnifies into chords of exaltation Wardour's death struggle among the ice floes of the Arctic. It is not strange that in the fantasy from which imagination is born Dickens should dream of a prisoner bitterly immured for years and at last set free, of a love serenely consummated and a despairing love triumphantly rising to noble heights of surrender. "I have so far verified what is done and suffered in these pages," he was later to write in the Preface to the novel, "as that I have certainly done and suffered it all myself." The statement was true. These emotions were his; he had known and suffered them all.

This is not to declare that Dr. Manette, Charles Darnay, and Sydney Carton are all self-portraits, or that Lucie Manette is a portrayal of Ellen Ternan. What the persons in the story do reflect as a group and in their several relations to the main situations of the story are the various individual aspects of Dickens' emotional dilemmas: his longing for an ideal love, his haunting fear that he might never find it, his anguished sense of the grandeur of renunciation, his personal rebellion against the imprisoning codes of society, and, rising above these, his impersonal rebellion against all the frustrations and miseries that society inflicted upon mankind.

Dr. Manette's imprisonment, above all, is both a personal and a social symbol. "Recalled to Life" Dickens once thought of calling the tale; but though Dr. Manette is recalled to life by love, he emerges from the Bastille frightfully mutilated in spirit and but slowly capable of achieving an unstable integration. In this way Dr. Manette embodies the hidden pain of the debtors' prison and the blacking warehouse which Dickens locked away in his memory, and Dr. Manette's solitude the deprivation of loving companionship to which Dickens had felt himself condemned. But, more than that, Dr.

Manette also stands for all those other sufferings that Dickens shared in his heart—the despair of those victims of workhouse "bastilles," the miseries of emaciated toilers condemned to hard labor in factories like jails, the anguish of wronged and deserted children. Can such evils ever be righted, such sufferings ever be expiated? Can the Bastille prisoner ever be *recalled to life*? Can the past with all its dreadful weight of guilt and pain ever be blotted out? Will not wrong engender wrong, flaming in all the horrors of the Revolution, engulfing both the innocent and the guilty in a sacrificial cataclysm?

Of all these threads, from distant childhood, from the anguish of the preceding year, and from all the years between, personal bitternesses and impersonal indignations, all involved and intertwined with each other, the scarlet fabric of *A Tale of Two Cities* is woven.

Acceptable and Unacceptable Violence in *A Tale of Two Cities*

John Kucich

In the following article, noted Dickens scholar John Kucich, author of *Excess and Restraint in the Novels of Charles Dickens*, examines how Dickens used and developed the theme of violence in *A Tale of Two Cities*. In Kucich's view, Dickens wants his readers to sympathize with the plight of the exploited French masses, who yearn to be released from the burdens of custom and social class that oppress them. Yet when the members of the mob finally do rise up, Dickens portrays their "release from limits" as an unacceptable form of violence because it turns cruel and arbitrary, much like the cold, mechanical violence that had so long been perpetrated on them by the upper classes. By contrast, Kucich maintains, Sydney Carton's act of self-sacrifice in the finale is an acceptable form of violence because it has what all can agree are higher moral purposes—to save Lucie and her family and to redeem Carton's own wasted life. Carton's death scene may be melodramatic and extreme, says Kucich, but it is a form of extremism to which readers respond with understanding and empathy.

After years of neglect, *A Tale of Two Cities* has probably become the most vigorously defended of Dickens' works. Recently, we have had numerous apologies for the novel that have uncovered its psychological complexities, its historical relevance, and the subtleties of its style with remarkable acuity. All of these critiques reveal that Dickens' novel is more sophisticated and more rewarding than has often been recognized. And yet, all of them seem to conclude that the novel ultimately fails in an important way ... [namely that]

Excerpted from "The Purity of Violence: *A Tale of Two Cities*" by John Kucich, *Dickens Studies Annual*, vol. 8 (1980), pp. 119-34. Reprinted by permission of AMS Press, New York, N.Y.

Sydney Carton's Christ-like martyrdom ... remains artificial, inadequate, and even embarrassing. This constant dissatisfaction with the ending implies that the fundamental problem for readers of *A Tale of Two Cities* is not the novel's general framework of ideas; the more serious problem is the novel's inability to provide an ethical or an analytical resolution—a useful resolution—to the social and psychological problems it announces, and its apparent willingness to submerge those problems in the stagey, emotionally charged but intellectually vapid crescendoes of melodrama. In other words, what we have here is a problem with narrative mode: it is the form of the novel that troubles modern readers, that frustrates expectations generated by the rest of the novel.

At the risk of bringing us full circle back to the grounds of early complaints against *A Tale of Two Cities*, I suggest that the serious uses of melodrama in the novel must be stressed if we are to understand its aesthetic wholeness. Spawned by Wilkie Collins' melodrama, *The Frozen Deep*, Dickens' novel has the play's emotional excessiveness at its very core, and any attempt to clarify the novel's thematic structure must therefore take up the challenge of that excessiveness. Recent studies have shown that debating melodrama's legitimacy as a literary mode is less profitable than articulating the ends that melodrama tries to achieve, if only in the interest of broadening our notions about the possible—and impossible—goals of narrative structure. In the case of *A Tale of Two Cities*, Dickens' novelistic goals depend heavily upon his melodramatic plot. In my view, the non-rational impulses behind melodrama develop a crucial authorial intention: Dickens' novel consistently works toward an escape from the realm of the analytical, the ethical, and the useable altogether. Instead, the novel investigates and defends desires for irrational extremity that it satisfies finally in Carton's chaste suicide. Dickens' attitude toward the role of emotional excess in human life, which is elaborately defined as the work unfolds, logically carries the novel away from orderly, intellectually apprehendable resolutions toward a more dynamic goal: the staging of acceptable—as opposed to cruel—violence.

A DESIRE TO BE RELEASED FROM LIMITS

A Tale of Two Cities is not a revolutionary novel, in the sense that it advocates political and social revolt, but it does dramatize a pressing, fundamental human need for liberating change of the most extreme kind. Dickens' novel is an enactment of human needs for an extreme release from many different kinds of confinement, and, in these terms, the novel's crucial development is a subtle change in the way violence can be valued as a vehicle for such release. That is to say, general needs for a victory over repression, which the novel embodies as a desire for violence, are purified as they are moved from the social context of the novel into the personal one: the revolutionaries' problematical desires for freedom are translated into acceptable terms by the good characters in their own struggles for freedom, and they are focused finally in the "pure" self-violence of Sydney Carton, which liberates him from self-hatred. In an abstract sense, what this means finally is that the novel's symbolic logic affirms Carton's initial tendencies toward an internal kind of violence—his dissipation—under the guise of his later, moral "conversion.". . . By reexamining Dickens' attitude toward excess and violence throughout the novel, we can begin to see why Carton's fate is unavoidable.

A non-specific, primary desire for a radical release from limits dominates the very texture of Dickens' novel. The famous opening paragraphs of the novel launch this movement toward release, articulating frustrated desires for extremity by way of parodying the desire of the historical imagination to erupt beyond the limits of conventional significance. Mixing the historian's typical desire to proclaim the extremity of his own elected period with undermining hints of the fundamental "sameness" of all ages, Dickens' much-quoted, much-sentimentalized opening catalogues the extremes of 1775 in a series of superlatives that cancel each other out: "It was the best of times, it was the worst of times, it was the age of wisdom, it was the age of foolishness, it was the epoch of belief, it was the epoch of incredulity . . ." (I, 1). Despite themselves, these terms fail to produce a difference in meaning; instead, each term merely tends to produce its opposite, and to be bounded by it. In this way, the opening catalogue of extremes comments more on the needs of the historical imagination— and on those of the novelist—than on the actual tenor of any particular age. It emphasizes desires for extremity at the same time that it frustrates them. As he levels extremes, the narrator even claims that his own chosen epoch is not actually different from the present one—giving greater emphasis to his debunking satire—but that "in short, the period was so far like the present period, that some of its noisiest authorities insisted on its being received, for good or for evil, in the superlative degree of comparison only." Far from being extreme, the age is actually in the grip of a repetitive sameness in its very desire to be excessive. . . .

SYDNEY CARTON'S CRISIS

The pathetic desire for extremity within history introduces more successful desires for upheaval on the part of characters. In the beginning, for example, Sydney Carton's dissipation is presented as the result of a metaphysical [spiritual] crisis over limitations, and not as the vulgarity of the idle bum: Carton feels imprisoned by the banality of economic survival. Referring to himself as a "drudge," Carton . . . flaunts his lack of economic sense: "Bless you, *I* have no business" (II, 4), he tells Lorry. In keeping with this violation of the code of self-interest, Carton had always instinctively done work for others rather than for himself in school; and, professionally, he does all his work so that Stryver, and not himself, may claim the credit and prosper. Carton's utter intellectual competence to lead a successful, if ordinary, life gives point to his rejection of self-concern, and defines it as a choice, however unconscious he may be of his own motives and however much such a choice is painful, bringing along with it the anonymity of self-abandonment. And, if Stryver and Lorry are examples of what success means, then Carton's comparative genuineness—his freedom from the rigidities of both aggression and repression—depends on his refusal to value worldly success. . . .

Despite the disapproval of other characters, the reader may find Carton's carelessness and his reckless honesty refreshing. Carton's dissipation is somehow "pure" precisely because it is free of self-interest. From the very beginning, Dickens forces the reader to discriminate between the popular judgment about Carton's degeneracy and the possibility of his having hidden merits, often by putting his condemnations of Carton into the wrong mouths. After all, it is the ugly mob, feasting like flies on Darnay's trail, that finds Carton's appearance disreputable, and it is Jerry Cruncher, after his vulgarity has been established, who observes: "I'd hold half a guinea that *he* don't get no law work to do. Don't look like the sort of one to get any, do he?" (II, 3). But Carton's supe-

riority to the crowd very soon emerges through his intensified powers of perception: "Yet, this Mr. Carton took in more
of the details of the scene than he appeared to take in; for
now, when Miss Manette's head dropped upon her father's
breast, he was the first to see it, and to say audibly: 'Officer!
look to that young lady. Help the gentleman to take her out.
Don't you see she will fall!'" The mark of Carton's genius is
this very ability to penetrate to the most important, the most
essential levels—to see beyond the limited vision of others,
or to say what others dare not say. In other words, Carton appeals to us through his freedom from convention and from
constraint. Thus, his success at Darnay's trial is a single,
bold, imaginative stroke, one that Stryver calls "a rare point"
(II, 5). . . . In contrast, then, to the other good characters,
whose lives are ruled by restraints of one kind or another,
and despite our sense that we must disapprove of him, Carton stands out as the most vividly authentic character in the
novel. Even in the love plot, Carton confides in Lucie more
honestly than the others: Darnay conceals from Lucie his intended trip to France, and Manette tries to conceal from her
his instinctual jealousy of Darnay. In the reader's eyes, Carton momentarily has a more intimate relationship with
Lucie than either Darnay or Manette, for the reader sees
Carton "open his heart" to her in the pivotal confession
scene, the only scene in which a man expresses himself pas-
sionately to Lucie. . . .

SYMPATHY FOR THE MOB SOON SOURS

Our ambivalent attitude toward Carton, then, is only an
index of the generally problematic nature of almost any violated limits. By being political, generational, sexual, and
vaguely misanthropic, desires for release in this novel acquire a kind of generality that transcends their local mani-
festations: such desires seem fundamentally human, while,
at the same time, they seem ultimately threatening. The
novel makes clear that while a desire for the destruction of
psychological and social limitations may be profoundly
human, it is always related to a desire for the destruction of
restrictive personal identity in violence and in death. . . .

On the one hand, in the initial stages of the revolution in
France, it is difficult not to sympathize with the laboring
class's pursuit of freedom through violence. Occasionally,
Dickens dwells on the mob's achievement of "human fellow-

ship" through their uprising, and stresses the sympathetic unity of the oppressed people: "Not before dark night did the men and women come back to the children, wailing and breadless. Then, the miserable bakers' shops were beset by long files of them, patiently waiting to buy bad bread; and while they waited with stomachs faint and empty, they beguiled the time by embracing one another on the triumphs of the day, and achieving them again in gossip. Gradually, these strings of ragged people shortened and frayed away; and then poor lights began to shine in high windows, and slender fires were made in the streets, at which neighbours cooked in common, afterwards supping at their doors" (II, 22). Then, too, the bursting wine cask scene, which mingles the sympathetic energy of a well-deserved holiday with ominous hints about the ultimate form of excessive "holiday" energy—the desire for blood, a word that someone writes into the wall in wine—also has the effect of linking the mob's exuberant expenditure of energy with Carton's drunkenness....

On the other hand, of course, the meaning of rebellion in France soon sours. Our reaction to the "Carmagnole" [the rebels' violent dance] cannot be the same as our reaction to the crowd that dammed up flowing wine in the cobblestones. The scenes of violence are carefully built up to repel us gradually, and it is difficult to specify at what particular point we lose sympathy with the rebels. But it soon becomes clear that the mob's struggle for justice is totally outstripped by their brute satisfaction in the violence of dominance. Hence, although the mob's struggle has its roots in oppression and therefore takes our sympathy, the novel jolts us into a recognition of the form taken by the mob's desire for liberation—its inevitable tendency to congeal in cruelty, and to project what was once a "pure," disinterested violence outward against others....

PURE VERSUS TAINTED VIOLENCE

In *A Tale of Two Cities* [two] forms of violence are personified and set at war with each other. The purity of self-violence clearly belongs at first to the lower classes, who "held life as of no account, and were demented with a passionate readiness to sacrifice it" (II, 21). Thus, the concrete effects of the revolutionaries' violence as an annihilation of their humanity—and, therefore, a violation of their human limitations—are actualized before us: we witness the transformation of rational figures like the Defarge couple into maddened beasts during the storming of the Bastille. Furthermore, to emphasize the "unnatural" and "non-human" element in the revolutionaries' passion, Dickens made their spokesperson a woman, since, in Dickens' world, the supreme disruption of normal expectations about human nature is an absence of tenderness in women. In the Parisian violence, even La Guillotine is female. And to heighten this effect, Madame Defarge's knitting in service of violence is set in sharp contrast to Lucie Manette's "golden thread" of pacification and harmony, as well as to the "domestic arts" that Lucie had learned in Madame Defarge's France. Most importantly, this yearning for the pure release of self-violence is identified as the ultimate form of desire for freedom through the good characters: Darnay, on his last night in prison, becomes fascinated with the guillotine—he has "a strange besetting desire to know what to do when the time came; a desire gigantically disproportionate to the few swift moments to which it referred; a wondering that was more like the wondering of some other spirit within his, than his own" (III, 3). . . .

The liberating intentions behind the lower classes' violence, however, are only a response to the repressive image of non-human freedom and "represented" violence that define the power of the class of Monseigneur. Instead of being defined through overt acts of violence, life among the upper classes revolves around static representations of their non-humanity—emblems of their willingness to violate human limits. The Marquis' own non-humanity marks itself in his freedom from emotion—the narrator at one point describes his appearance as being "a fine mask" (II, 9), and his face is compared to the stone faces of his gargoyles. . . .

There is violence among the Marquis' class, of course, but it is colder, and has a clear function as a representation: that is, their violence is merely an occasional symbol of the mastery of the rich, since it proves their right to waste lives if they choose to—the lives of the lower orders. When the Marquis asserts that running down children with his carriage is a right of his station, he takes no passionate satisfaction from the killing; he takes only a numbed confirmation of his status. Initially, when the rebels in *A Tale of Two Cities* kill, they kill in passion, while the rich kill as spectacle—as, for example, when the royal government executes the murderer of the Marquis and leaves him hanging forty feet in the air. . . .

[The] horror of *A Tale of Two Cities* is this: at the point when the revolutionaries stop short of their own willingness to brave death and attempt to make their release permanent and meaningful in the form of a Republic, they trap themselves in the reified form of diverted violence—the petty, mechanical, and cruel contortions of human rivalry. We lose sympathy for the rebels when they lose sight of their limitless freedom—their "pure" release—and become trapped in their own revenge, thus imitating their oppressors. The very name of Madame Defarge's companion is "The Vengeance," and Madame Defarge undercuts herself through an ironic imitation: she dedicates herself to destroying the innocent Darnay family just as her own innocent family was destroyed. More disturbingly, for Madame Defarge, as for the rest of the revolutionaries, passionate revenge gives way to the invention of spurious rivalry, the murder of innocent victims. The purely mechanical quality of this imitative violence is underscored by the ominous note of historical destiny in this novel: the continuous references to things "running their courses" and the metaphors of echoing footsteps and approaching thunderstorms. In Dickens' novel, the "pure" wish for release always becomes tainted when it is diverted away from the self, and when the limits that are violated become the limits of others. . . . In fact, the social and personal histories of *A Tale of Two Cities* converge on the theme of release that is trapped in rivalry: the novel dramatizes the failure even of Dickens' heroes to escape the structure of rivalry in their efforts to achieve release. In this novel, suppressing the rivalry inherent in release is not simply inadequate: it is elaborately examined as a strategy that fails. . . .

TWO CRUCIAL CHARACTER CONFLICTS

In both of the crucial relationships among the good characters, inherent violence is only imperfectly suppressed, and finally emerges—even against the characters' wills—as rivalry. In the first conflict, Dr. Manette's voluntary suppression of his opposition to Darnay—which is both political, on account of the novel's germinal incident in France, and sexual, because they are locked in a relationship of natural, generational rivalry—is itself dangerous. Often, it sinks him back into the corrosive oblivion of work as he tries to screen out his jealousy. Lorry wonders "whether it is good for Dr.

Manette to have that suppression always shut up within him" (II, 6). Even worse though, despite all his attempts to overcome it, Manette's involuntary rivalry with Darnay is mercilessly actualized by events. Manette's very attempts to save Darnay from the revolutionary tribunal are compromised by a dangerous, potential one-upsmanship in his performance: "[H]e was proud of his strength. 'You must not be weak, my darling,' he remonstrated; 'don't tremble so. I have saved him'" (III, 6). This one-upsmanship is stressed by the Doctor's dependence on the rivalrous mob, which is devoted to Darnay's death. And, more significantly, the production of the document recounting the story of the Peasant Family realizes Manette's rivalry in a deadly way. . . .

In the second, more important rivalry, the one between Sydney Carton and Charles Darnay, the conditions of the rivalry are again involuntary: the two characters simply look alike, which stings Carton with a sense of his inferiority. Carton's metaphysical urges for violent release—like the desire of Manette for freedom, and like the desires of the lower class in this novel for liberation—is trapped in his envy of a rival, Darnay. Carton even selects his rival as the man who most completely displays a willingness to risk life, and who receives recognition for it: "Is it worth being tried for one's life," he says, "to be the object of such sympathy and compassion, Mr. Darnay?" (II, 4) As a consequence, Carton's general bitterness about the limitations of his life focus themselves in this competition with Darnay for the clearest claim to violent self-expenditure and selflessness.

What makes the second relationship more interesting than the first is that Carton is finally able to satisfy his drive toward release in a morally legitimate way precisely through the structure of rivalry. Carton's "self-sacrifice," far from transcending structures of rivalry, actually operates within them. The will-to-power here is clear: Carton takes over Darnay's very handwriting and uses it to address an intimate message to Lucie, one that Darnay cannot understand or share; he refers to the unconscious Darnay as "me"; he envisions the surviving couple as "not more honoured and held sacred in each other's soul, than I was in the souls of both" (III, 15); and he pictures Darnay's own son named after him, along with a grandson also named after himself, who comes back to France solely for the purpose of hearing the Carton story. The crowning irony in Carton's violation of

Darnay's identity and his claim to Lucie's admiration is that Carton is the one who projects the others' future in the last paragraphs of the novel, while both Manette and Darnay are lying in a coach, impotent and unconscious. . . .

Carton's sacrifice is meant to be compelling because it is superior to Darnay's, since Darnay's death would have been involuntary, and because it seems to make him "more worthy" of Lucie. Carton achieves a transcendent "meaning" only by demonstrating a greater willingness to face death. At the same time, however, Carton does not appropriate for himself any undesirable associations with mastery because he makes his self-expenditure complete. By losing his life, Carton annihilates self-interest. Moreover, besides the totality of his loss, Carton also nullifies any appropriation of recognition that he might conceivably desire by refusing to reveal his sacrifice to anyone while it is in preparation. Unlike Dr. Manette's ostentatious rescue of Darnay, Carton's proceeds in secret. He informs no one—not even Lorry—and he tells Lucie only in a note meant to be opened later, so that she would know that his life had not been "wantonly" thrown away. The awesome thing about Carton's death is just this: that he goes through it alone—he even dies under someone else's name. . . . And, ultimately, the violent aspect of Carton's "suicide" is redeemed through the preservation of Darnay and his family. Radical self-violence is balanced with meaning derived from its being put to temporal, conservative use. As an action, Carton's is the only violent release in the novel that can claim the readers' unqualified assent, since even actions like Dr. Manette's liberation from prison or Darnay's liberation from his English trial immediately cause new, unavoidable problems of rivalry. . . .

AN UNDISGUISED DESIRE FOR DEATH

If the conclusion of *A Tale of Two Cities* seems contrived, Dickens is well aware of at least one side of the contrivance: the rivalrous aspect of Carton's act is clearly articulated. Readers offended by the "simple-mindedness" of Carton's crucifixion can take solace in Dickens' awareness of this dimension to the act. At the same time, however, Dickens clearly intended the conclusion to move his readers unequivocally, as only the magnitude of death dramatized as a human desire could move them. What makes this ending melodramatic is not simply Carton's death, but his undisguised *desire* for death. We are well-protected against this desire in our normal lives, and, as Peter Brooks points out, one reason for critical embarrassment with the form of melodrama may very well be melodrama's refusal to censor itself. For this reason, whether the conclusion of *A Tale of Two Cities* moves or embarrasses us, the reason is the same: Dickens has presented us with an image of an explicitly desired violation of human limits, one that is presented as the only possible escape from the twin mechanisms of rivalry and repressed violence. In some of the later novels, Dickens attempts to make the liberation of self-violence possible through an intensified consciousness of death. . . . But, in *A Tale of Two Cities*, the synthesis of ultimate release and survival takes place only in the unstated relationship between Sydney Carton's death and the reader's awareness of that death's significance.

Recurring Metaphors of Water and Death by Drowning

Garrett Stewart

The following essay is an excerpt from the intriguing book *Death Sentences: Styles of Dying in British Fiction*, by Garrett Stewart, professor of English at the University of California, Santa Barbara. In his careful analysis of Dickens's *A Tale of Two Cities*, Stewart singles out the many symbolic references to flowing, often rushing water and to death by drowning. This imagery ranges from rivers of blood symbolized by streams of wine from a broken cask, to the "living sea" of the angry Parisian crowds, to the "current" of death stalking the streets of revolutionary Paris. According to Stewart, Dickens was fascinated by images of death and his novels are replete with death scenes, including a number involving drowning.

While strolling through Paris early one morning late in his career and his life, Dickens noticed a motley procession turning round in front of Notre-Dame. Thinking it to be a christening or a marriage, those two transitional rites that figure with such prominence in his fiction, he soon discovered it related instead to the third. "Having never before chanced upon this initiation," he joined an eager crowd watching an anonymous corpse being delivered to the morgue. What he imagined others seeing in the person of this corpse affords a catalogue of the satirized vanities and selfish anxieties that so often attend death in his fiction. More to the point for the stylistic maneuvers by which death is necessarily rendered in narrative, Dickens notes in particular that all the stares of the crowd, his own included, "concurred in possessing the one underlying expression of *looking at something that could not return a look*.". . .

THE FLOODGATES OF BLOODSHED

It cannot too often be said that in his fictional practice, as well as in such a biographical anecdote, Dickens was doubly a man of his epoch: obsessed by death, fascinated by its demands upon articulation [speaking or writing about it]. To write of dying is often to stretch language's binding temporality—binding in the sense of both style's obligations and its ligatures—toward and across the point of threatened severance. This is frequently achieved in Dickens's fiction by a kind of calculus of decreasing intervals approaching the unknown . . . [for example, in] the gradually developed metaphors of death by water in *A Tale of Two Cities* (1859). These figures gather toward and help gloss the sacrificial death of the hero [Sydney Carton], dispatched of course by the blade and not by drowning, as that death is redeemed in and by narrative. One of the first full-scale renderings of the Parisian scene under the Reign of Terror comes to us filtered through its horrific revelation to the mind of Jarvis Lorry: "All this was seen in a moment, as the vision of a drowning man, or any human creature at any very great pass, could see a world if it were there" (III, 3). Drowning is Dickens's definitive metaphor for this rite of perceptual passage, with the noun "vision" suspended in the periodic sentence long enough to stand for both effect and cause, vista and empowered eyesight. Fortified by countless later analogies to the Terror as a bloody Flood come again, this simile foresees the visionary acuity that the hero himself achieves when he drowns symbolically in the tidal heave of revolutionary violence.

To place Sydney Carton's sacrifice within this larger historical context, we need to return to the first retributive scene of death in the novel, characterized by Dickens's usual verbal tension and ingenuity. The assassination of the vicious Marquis St. Evrémonde, portrayed as the initiating act of the revolution, leads at the public and private level directly to the execution of Carton, scapegoat of the Terror. The Marquis is only found dead by narration, not watched die. . . . With the Marquis's affectless sly ferocity and his heart of stone, it is only appropriate for prose to discover him unruffled by death, yet already stiffened in its aftermath. The word *death* is never mentioned, but the Gorgon of the ancestral mansion has found "the stone face for which it had waited through about two hundred years.". . .

Rage swollen to the breaking point, the floodgates of

bloodshed are now thrown open. This figurative sense of the nightmare to follow is no dead metaphor in the novel. Murderous impulse is repeatedly imaged as the impetus of inundation—as in those rivers of blood for which that broken wine cask in the famous fifth chapter is a prototype. The carnage grows intoxicating and inexorable. With the return of the marquis to a stone-cold gargoyle in the dead edifice of his world, Dickens begins the transformation from historical time into apocalyptic time, the fixating of the former with moribund stasis [stillness of death] along with the release of the latter into a set of images derived from the Flood in Genesis. This is the ultimate manner, too, in which this first dramatic death scene in the novel is channeled directly into, and filtered clean by, the sacrificial (and literal) decapitation of the hero, Carton, where the apocalyptic images of flood that follow from the marquis's murder are internalized as the private mind's "drowning" vision. It is a vision compressed and, in the hero's access to narrative grace, prophetic.

A TIDE SWIFT AND DEEP

In a novel that drops in passing an apocalyptic hint about the Day of Judgment when the "ocean is . . . to give up its dead" (II, 2), the explicit imagery of flood and drowning begins innocuously enough as a double turn of phrase in that very chapter, "The Wine-Shop," that gives us in symbol the first overspill of revolutionary desperation. The underprovided lamps of the Saint Antoine quarter are seen there to provide merely "dim wicks" that "swung in a sickly manner overhead, as if they were at sea" (I, 5). The simile is then shifted over to idiom and to omen: "Indeed they were at sea, and the ship and crew were in peril of tempest." From that point on the metaphor rarely lets up. Building toward the outbreak of violence, one chapter closes in an eightfold . . . spate of clauses begun with the rush of literal water and sped quickly to metaphor: "The water of the fountain ran, the swift river ran, the day ran into evening, so much life in the city ran into death according to rule, time and tide waited for no man," and so on as "all things ran their course" (II, 7). It is not long before the "living sea" of mob violence "rose, wave on wave, depth on depth," a vast and "resistless . . . ocean" (II, 21). The irreversible momentum of this flood runs straight into the title of the subsequent chapter, "The Sea Still Rises," and from there into the third book, where the "current" of death continues to "rend" and "strew" (III, 6) its victims.

By this third book, however, the figures are undergoing a certain internalization as well, so that Darnay in prison, hearing the distant "swell that rose" against him, also finds "scraps tossing and rolling upward from the depth of his mind" (III, 1). His double, Carton, tending to see his own life as a merely troubled, restless, superficial swirl in the torrent

---

MR. QUILP'S GRUESOME END

In addition to his frequent use of metaphorical drowning, Dickens sometimes depicted real drownings in his novels. One of the most memorable and graphic of all Dickensian death scenes, excerpted here, is from The Old Curiosity Shop, *in which the mean, unscrupulous Daniel Quilp finally receives his just rewards in dark river waters.*

He staggered and fell—and next moment was fighting with the cold dark water!

For all its bubbling up and rushing in his ears, he could hear the knocking at the gate again—could hear a shout that followed it—could recognise the voice. For all his struggling and plashing, he could understand that they . . . were all but looking on, while he was drowned; that they were close at hand, but could not make an effort to save him. . . . He answered the shout—with a yell, which seemed to make the hundred fires that danced before his eyes tremble and flicker, as if a gust of wind had stirred them. It was of no avail. The strong tide filled his throat, and bore him on, upon its rapid current.

Another mortal struggle, and he was up again, beating the water with his hands, and looking out, with wild and glaring eyes that showed him some black object he was drifting close upon. The hull of a ship! He could touch its smooth and slippery surface with his hand. One loud cry now—but the resistless water bore him down before he could give it utterance, and, driving him under it, carried away a corpse.

It toyed and sported with its ghastly freight, now bruising it against the slimy piles, now hiding it in mud or long rank grass, now dragging it heavily over rough stones and gravel, now feigning to yield it to its own element, and in the same action luring it away, until, tired of the ugly plaything, it flung it on a swamp—a dismal place where pirates had swung in chains, through many a wintry night—and left it there to bleach.

---

of history, is more ironically self-conscious about the appli-
cation of tidal analogies before an actual river: "The strong
tide, so swift, so deep, and certain, was like a congenial
friend" in which he sees glassed a replica of his own relation
to it, "watching an eddy that turned and turned purposeless,
until the stream absorbed it, and carried it on to the sea.—
Like me!" (III, 9). Just before that self-accusatory internal
echo ("sea" / "me"), Carton's "chain" of reverie leads him
back to thoughts of his father's funeral, retrieving its recited
sacred text "like a rusty old ship's anchor from the deep."
The tacit idiom "chain of association" is thus aptly literalized
as the recovery of a previous being far submerged in the internal tides of mind. For this man who had once characterized himself to Lucie Manette as "like one who died young"
(II, 13), the memory of his father's funeral is a partial resurrection of his earlier self coincident with the now recalled
words, "I am the Resurrection and the Life." A confession of
Carton's previous psychic burial is cannily unlocked in this
same paragraph within the most straightforward of idioms:
"Long ago, when he had been famous among his earliest
competitors as a youth of great promise, he had *followed his
father to the grave*. His mother had died, years before" (my
emphasis on Dickens's funereal duplicity). In a single
phrase we find the justification for all that macabre comedy
about grave robbing that centers around Jerry Cruncher as
Resurrection Man. It is Carton, not only orphaned but in-
terred, who must be "recalled to life" again in a lifting out of
himself that raises him to the sacrificial scaffold, regardless
of any further elevation by death itself.

THE OCEAN CLEANSES

Lazarus-like, making good on the first person of the Lord's
annunciation, Carton ascends not through but to his death
scene, from the stilled "deep" of his humanity into that public storm where "fifty-two were to roll that afternoon on the
life-tide of the city to the boundless everlasting sea" (III, 13).
Even the figurative verb there is a threefold pun compound-
ing the oceanic metaphor of death with its literal cause and
effect in the remorseless roll of the condemned and the con-
sequent roll of their heads under the guillotine. For the man
whose mother had died in his infancy, his goal, shared with
the seamstress whom he has befriended in his last hours,
will be to rejoin the "Universal Mother" across the untra-

versable distance of death's "dark highway." It is a distance implicated in the interval of a nearby play on words, Carton and the girl hoping "to repair home together, and to rest in her bosom" (III, 15), where the imagined journey to their long home overtakes and includes the sense of a "reparation" for all earthly losses. . . .

After a paragraph reiterating the text of "I am the Resurrection and the Life," we pass to another elided interval: "The murmuring of many voices, the upturning of many faces, the pressing on of many footsteps in the outskirts of the crowd, so that it swells forward in a mass like one great heave of water, all flashes away. Twenty-Three.". . . The phrase "flashes away" is not only a formulaic description of drowning quite common in literary treatments . . . but it is also an echo of that earlier murder of Madame Defarge and the sacrificial impairment of Miss Pross: "'I feel,' said Miss Pross, 'as if there had been a flash and a crash, and that crash was the last thing I should ever hear in this life'" (III, 14). Locution there for an explosive burst of light, "flash" has gone from noun of ignition to a verb of extinguishment across a pattern of mortal displacement captured by Dickensian prose at the level of echoing monosyllables. For what Miss Pross, clinging to Madame Defarge "with more than the hold of a drowning woman," saw and heard, the murderousness of the world turned against itself, is what Carton will no longer be made to suffer, having taken the violence unto himself as his own liberating fate. The canceling "crash" that follows the earlier gunpowder "flash" has become the guillotine's twice-repeated "Crash!" by which the whole scene of terror, in a chiastic inversion of the earlier death scene and its rhetoric, is finally "flashed" away for Carton, at the moment when the ferocious ocean of hate both overtakes and cleanses him.

Public Execution in
A Tale of Two Cities

Catherine Gallagher

In addition to being an art form, the nineteenth-century Victorian novel was also a social phenomenon, a public forum that by various techniques revealed otherwise private characters, acts, and thoughts to the general public. The most common of these techniques was the omniscient, or all-knowing, narrator, who could lay bare the most private aspects of life for all to examine. Thus, as literary scholar Catherine Gallagher points out in the following essay, the novel was analogous, or comparable, to many of the public social practices depicted in its own pages. Gallagher argues that public execution as portrayed in *A Tale of Two Cities* graphically exposes a person's privacy to the crowd's scrutiny. And although Dickens abhorred and often spoke out against public executions, he performed the same sort of blatant annihilation of privacy in his role as omniscient narrator of his novels.

For the past several years readers have been discovering that Victorian novels can be as ironically self-reflective as any novels. Now that they are expected to, Thackeray, Dickens, and George Eliot reveal the fictitiousness of their fictions, the constructed nature of their constructions, the worldliness of their worlds. . . . One of the primary techniques of Victorian self-reflectiveness that has lately attracted attention is the insertion into the novel of analogues [things or ideas that are very similar] for novelistic narration, analogues that expose the constructing operations of the narrator even as he or she pretends to be passively mirroring an objective reality. . . .

   This essay links the question of what the narrative conceals by providing doubles for itself to the issue of the connection

Excerpted from "The Duplicity of Doubling in *A Tale of Two Cities*" by Catherine Gallagher, *Dickens Studies Annual*, vol. 12 (1983), pp. 125-44. Reprinted by permission of AMS Press, New York, N.Y.

between the novel and the social phenomena it purports to represent. Like all historical novels, *A Tale of Two Cities* advertises itself as a record of events that had their own separate existence outside of the novel. And like realist novels in general, it can accommodate a real deal of self-referentiality without relinquishing its claim to represent an independent reality. Indeed, *A Tale of Two Cities*, like many nineteenth-century novels, often achieves its self-reflectiveness just by calling attention to itself as mere representation. By presenting itself as simple representation, a thing whose very thingness is secondary . . . the novel conceals an aspect of itself; it conceals the fact that it is itself a kind of social practice. By drawing its content from social phenomena that are at once independent realities and analogues for novelistic narration, the novel gets us to focus alternately on what it is *about* and on how it accomplishes its representational effects. In the very act of giving us these alternative perspectives, the novel obscures its deeply social roots and functions. But the critic can uncover what the novel seeks to bury if she refuses to limit herself to the perspectives of the text itself, if she is willing to regard the novel as one among a number of historical phenomena, to investigate the separate but competing social functions of the novel and the phenomena it takes as its dark doubles.

The issue of analogues, metaphors, or doubles for narration and the issue of the social functions of fiction, then, are dealt with here as a single issue, an issue inseparable from larger topics in nineteenth-century social history. To demonstrate this unity, I will discuss . . . the English public execution . . . presented in *A Tale of Two Cities* as [a] monstrous violator of the realm of the private. As such, [it] might seem to threaten the very foundations of the nineteenth-century novel, a genre that grows out of and depends on a high valuation of the private and domestic realms. . . . The transgression of the very public/private boundary created and valued by the novel can be detected everywhere in Dickens' novels. The wish to take the house-tops off, to render the private observable, is the wish informing the very existence of the omniscient narrator. . . .

Even as the narrator suggests that exposure can be the work of a good spirit, expelling hidden evils and creating light and order, he reminds us that it is nevertheless a transgression, and, consequently, within the novel's structure of values, akin to the work of a demon. How can the novel conceal this side of its own need to reveal and expose; how can the novelist reassure himself and his readers that he is in league with the good spirit, that his operations are benign? One way to suppress the fear that novelistic omniscience verges on the demonic is to provide, within the novel, an alternative version of the will to omniscience, one that is clearly destructive, preferably murderous or ghoulish, so that by contrast, the narrator's activities will seem restrained and salutary. Execution ... perform[s] precisely this function in *A Tale of Two Cities.*

THE MOMENT OF SUFFERING AND DEATH

Consider ... the public execution, and consider it, for a moment, independently of the novel to get a sense of why Dickens was attracted to it. No event was better suited to render the private public, to expose the intimate in the interests of public order. In its most obvious sense, this would be true of all public executions, for by definition they expose to full public view a moment that was becoming more and more intensely private as the nineteenth century wore on, the moment of fatal suffering and death. That exposure should remind us of the historical links between public executions and those other ritual inversions of public and private: human sacrifice and carnival. Furthermore, when we consider the physical details of hanging, the type of execution used in England seems calculated to maximize the exposure of the dying victim. The erection of the penis and the evacuation of the bowels are among such details, and hanging, up until quite late in the Victorian period, was a slow-working method; the drop was short, and the body was left, fully visible, to writhe and strangle for many minutes.

Moreover, as Dickens reminds us in *A Tale of Two Cities,* some crimes were punishable by even more intrusive forms of exposure. One of our earliest views of Charles Darnay renders him, through the ogreish anticipation of the crowd at his trial, a man literally turned inside out:

> The sort of interest with which this man was stared and breathed at, was not a sort that elevated humanity. Had he stood in peril of a less horrible sentence—had there been a chance of any one of its savage details being spared—by just so much would he have lost in his fascination. The form that was to be doomed to be so shamefully mangled, was the sight; the immortal creature that was to be so butchered and torn asunder, yielded the sensation.

Treason, you will recall, is the charge, and the penalty is an almost unimaginable mixing up of specular awareness and intense interiority, as the live sufferer is forced to watch the breaking open, pulling out and destruction of his own insides. To emphasize the extent of its violation, Dickens includes the full sentence:

> "Ah!" returned the man, with a relish; "he'll be drawn on a hurdle to be half hanged, and then he'll be cut down and sliced before his own face, and then his inside will be taken out and burnt while he looks on, and then his head will be chopped off, and he'll be cut into quarters. That's the sentence."

In these fairly obvious ways, then, the public execution, especially when accompanied by torture, can be seen as a nightmare of transparency, of publicly displaying what is hidden, intimate, secret, in the interests of creating social order and cohesion. Here is a collective longing for omniscience and power taking the most savage form imaginable. Here it is not just the walls or rooftops of the house that are ripped away, but the walls of the body itself. And thus Dickens' appalled references to several brutal executions at the outset of the novel establish the crucial differences between such practices and the novel's own will to transparency. Compared to the awful executions mentioned in chapter one and to Damiens's execution recounted later in detail, the novelist's methods of exposing the intimate are safe, sane, sanitary, and benevolent. They are safe because they do not entail that reversibility of violence dramatized in *A Tale of Two Cities*. . . . Penal reformers of the eighteenth and nineteenth centuries (and Dickens was such a reformer) feared that a population exposed to such a violent theater of punishment would become a violent population. This note is sounded early in *A Tale of Two Cities*, where we learn in the first chapter that the hangman's seemingly arbitrary activities only contribute further to the disorder and violence that can easily turn against the State, and keep turning and turning as they do in Dickens' portrayal of the French Revolution.

THE ALTERNATIVE OF THE PRIVATE EXECUTION

In contrast, the novelist may pry, spy, and expose the secret, the personal, but he manages to do these things while maintaining both propriety and privacy. Indeed, the very production and consumption of novels, as well as their contents, perpetuate the idea that the private can be made public, brought to light, and yet still be kept private. In this sense, Dickens' work as a novelist is of a piece with his work in reforming the law. The public execution, he argues, should give way to a procedure relying on a few witnesses and a lot of paperwork. As Dickens describes the procedure in a letter to the *Times* in 1849, the multitude of the crowd would be replaced by a multitude of pieces of writing:

> To attend the execution I would summon a jury of 24, to be called the Witness Jury, eight to be summoned on a low qualification, eight on a higher; eight on a higher still; so that it might fairly represent all classes of society. There should be present likewise, the governor of the gaol, the chaplain, the surgeon and other officers. All these should sign a grave and solemn form of certificate (the same in every case) on such a day on such an hour, in such a gaol, for such a crime, such a murderer was hanged in their sight. There should be another certificate from the officers of the prison that the person hanged was that person and no other; a third that the person was buried.

As in the novel itself, in the private execution, as Dickens called his imagined punishment, that which is private is given over to the power of the public, but the public executes its power privately.

Thus, the very form of the novel defines itself against the public execution, not only in spite of, but also because of their resemblances. This is especially true in *A Tale of Two Cities*, which establishes the public execution as one of its founding abominations. To take the public execution merely as a point of departure, however, is to ignore some of the more subtle ways in which the novel incorporates and depends on the institution of the public execution. To explore these further connections, I will need to discuss not the general institution of public executions, but certain peculiarities of English public executions. Thus far I have been talking as if the execution, both inside and outside the novel, consisted merely in the forcible exposure of the intimate sensations of the condemned person's body, but the English execution did two other things particularly well that the novel was supposed to do: it retrospectively narrated an individual life while it simultaneously created a sense of social cohesion and totality.

English executions differed from those of other nations in the degree of activity allowed the victim and his opportunities for autobiographical representation. The victim's first such opportunity was his trial, but many opportunities succeeded condemnation. There was, for example, the theatrical opportunity provided by the prison chapel service that took place on the Sunday before the execution. Here the Ordinary of Newgate, the prison chaplain, would deliver a sermon, not only to the condemned, but also to the crowds of people who would bribe their way in to see the condemned. Because they had an audience, the prisoners were very often rowdy during this service, intent on expressing themselves, and the Ordinary's record is crowded with complaints: Christopher Freeman, we learn, "behaved very undecently, laughed and seemed to make a mock of everything that was serious and regular." And Ann Mudd, the account tells, "Used to sing obscene songs, and talked very indecently," while Christopher Rawlings in the days before he was hanged busied himself in chapel by cutting off the tassels of the pulpit cushion. In addition to these small examples of self-dramatization, each condemned prisoner in Newgate was required to go through an autobiographical exercise. He was required to assist the Ordinary in making an *account* of his life. And there were frequently extraordinary struggles over these accounts. In the first place, the Ordinary as narrator often had difficulty subduing his rebellious characters. They would not always go along with his version of the plot. A historian of Newgate tells us,

> The Ordinary not only liked to have positive statements of guilt to the particular crime, but assent to a general range of immoral conduct. A story was told about Lorraine [an eighteenth-century Ordinary] and a young pickpocket about to be hanged. The Ordinary, expecting to hear the lad explain his sinful life in terms of Sabbath-breaking, lewd women or drink, was surprised when the boy insisted that he was innocent of them all, particularly the first since as a pickpocket he could never afford to miss a Sunday.

In the second place, prisoners often wanted to sell their stories to higher bidders outside the prison walls. They wrote their own manuscripts in secret and smuggled them out to high-paying publishers. Other prisoners simply tried to keep their secret until they were on the scaffold, where their last speech would reveal all. But even before they got to the scaffold, in the days when hanging took place at Tyburn, there were ample opportunities for making speeches about one's life. The procession sometimes made several pub stops and stops to visit friends; the condemned would get down and drink and talk over old times. Both during these stops and during other parts of the journey, the condemned gave blessings, kissed their children goodbye, cursed people, etc. Executions, in short, could turn into enacted autobiographies, which were supplemented by the many accounts of the life and crimes of the condemned that were being sold all along the route and at the place of execution. Such life histories of criminals were, of course, the immediate ancestors of the novel.

THE CROWDS THAT TURNED OUT TO WATCH

English executions were also unique in the extent to which they obscured the power of the State. They seem staged to create the illusion that a total society, not a single class or government, was executing a felon. What is more, in the eighteenth and nineteenth centuries, the people were not content to be represented symbolically through the crown at these events, but turned out themselves in huge and generally disorderly crowds that were nevertheless socially differentiated. Indeed, we might argue that, in a time when a sense of social totality was becoming increasingly difficult to achieve, the public execution was a reassuring representation of wholeness. Nowhere else would all strata of society display themselves in such numbers. Tickets were sold, and the wealthy would pay high prices for gallery seats. At public executions one could see the differentiated but nevertheless cohesive whole of eighteenth- and nineteenth-century England.

The public execution, then, in addition to enacting a personal narrative also provided a synoptic view [summary or overview] of society; the very two things the novel prided itself on doing. Indeed, the connection between the novelistic synoptic vision and the public hanging is explicit in a few of Dickens' novels. A famous early example of this connection is the death of Bill Sikes in *Oliver Twist*. Sikes's death admittedly is not technically an execution, but that makes it all the more revealing for my purposes, for it perfectly reproduces the submergence of the state in the English execution. It is the whole population of London, and not just the police, that brings Sikes to bay and causes him to hang himself—Sikes is on a rooftop attempting to let himself down, with a rope, into a ditch:

> The crowd had been hushed during these few moments, watching his motions and doubtful of his purpose, but the in-

> stant they perceived it and knew it was defeated, they raised
> a cry of triumphant execration to which all their previous
> shouting had been whispers. Again and again it rose. Those
> who were at too great a distance to know its meaning, took up
> the sound; it echoed and re-echoed; it seemed as though the
> whole city had poured its population out to curse him.
>
> On pressed the people from the front—on, on, on, in a strong
> struggling current of angry faces, with here and there a gath-
> ering torch to light them up, and show them out in all their
> wrath and passion. The houses on the opposite side of the
> ditch had been entered by the mob; sashes were thrown up,
> or torn bodily out; there were tiers and tiers of faces in every
> window; cluster upon cluster of people clinging to every
> house-top. Each little bridge (and there were three in sight)
> bent beneath the weight of the crowd upon it. Still the current
> poured on to find some nook or hole from which to vent their
> shouts, and only for an instant see the wretch.

This is the only time in the novel that the divided world of
the metropolis achieves wholeness, for Harry Maylie and
Mr. Brownlow are parts of the mob, which also includes the
poor and the criminal. . . . The roof-top here is the perch of
omniscience, but the synoptic moment is created and perceived only in the seconds before hanging.

Dickens also uses the moment of execution as the synoptic moment in *A Tale of Two Cities.* Here again the omniscience gained in the moment of Sydney Carton's execution,
a prophetic vision giving us a chronological panorama extending several generations into the future, is synonymous
with the narrator's omniscience.

EXECUTION AND SELF-EXECUTION ON THE STAGE

In sum, Dickens uses the public execution as a method of
defining, by contrast, the innocence of his own longing for
transparency and omniscience. However, he then incorporates the conventions of representation of the English execution into his narrative to achieve some of his most typically novelistic effects: the retrospective of Sydney Carton's
life, for example, and the prophetic synopsis of its close. This
incorporation, indeed, is an effort to absorb the functions of
the public execution and circumscribe them within the
novel. In the same letter to the *Times* in which Dickens re-
quested that the crowd be replaced by its representatives
(eight men from each social class) at executions, he expressed his hostility toward the theatrically autobiographical character of public executions. He recommends that all

elements of public entertainment be suppressed:

> [The] execution within the walls of the prison should be con-
> ducted with every terrible solemnity that careful considera-
> tion could devise. Mr. Calcraft the hangman . . . should be re-
> strained in his unseemly briskness, in his jokes, his oaths,
> and his brandy.

Moreover, even journalistic accounts publicizing the condemned are to be disallowed:

> From the moment of a murderer being sentenced to death, I
> would dismiss him to dread obscurity. . . . I would allow no
> curious visitors to hold any communication with him; I
> would place every obstacle in the way of his sayings and do-
> ings being served up in print on Sunday for the perusal of
> families.

The novelist alone, it seems, should be able to appropriate,
through representation, the functions of the execution. . . .

Consequently, in *A Tale of Two Cities* we have a clear illustration of how omniscient, novelistic narration came to
replace certain social practices of an earlier, more theatrical
society by temporarily assuming some essential functions of
those practices and then making itself an explicit contrast to
them. Of all nineteenth-century novelists, Dickens may have
been the most aware of the close bond between his own
works and the more public and theatrical practices they
were replacing. That may, in fact, be why we find in his
work the cleverest mechanisms of concealment. The mechanisms need to be clever, for the thing being concealed is, in
some ways, very obvious. The novel does not just record a
social transition; it enacts one.

That transition was perhaps most powerfully enacted,
paradoxically, on the Victorian stage itself, where Dickens,
in the last years of his life, added a new item to his repertoire
of public readings. He began doing the murder of Nancy and
death of Bill Sikes from *Oliver Twist*, and he reported that the
performances bore a strong resemblance to public executions: "There was a fixed expression of horror of me, all over
the theatre, which could not have been surpassed if I had
been going to be hanged. . . . It is quite a new sensation to be
executed with that unanimity." How can this final institutional exchange be explained? Was Dickens giving back to
the public, theatrical realm much of what he had appropri-
ated from it? Were these readings public confessions, disclosures of the novelist's guilty connection to the phenomena
he was displacing, as well as acts of reparation?

In answer to the first question, it must be pointed out that Dickens is here entering the realm of the theatrical, but only, after all, to modify it in the direction of the novelistic. His readings in general made a peculiarly non-theatrical use of the theater: with most of the stage darkened and draped, the solitary reader stood at the velvet-covered lectern reading the already familiar stories. No characters appeared, no scenes became visible; all was represented in words, realized only privately through the imaginative effort of each of the thousands of hearers. . . .

From this understanding of the readings in general, we may be able to derive the meaning of the violent *Oliver Twist* performances, which Dickens thought bore such a strong likeness to public executions. As in all of Dickens' readings, the performance called attention to its novelistic representational mode; there was no stage illusion. The simulated self-execution of Sikes took place only in the private space of the hearers' minds, while the shared experiences were of Dickens' voice and the spectacle of his self-presentation as narrator. The revelation here is of the novelist, not of the executed. In his performance, Dickens does not directly pretend to be Bill Sikes; he does not even take the risk of identification taken by a normal actor. Instead, Dickens plays the novelist, exposes himself as novelist. It is the anonymous revealer who is here revealed. Consequently, in these performances, the novelist proves that he is willing to expose himself, and his exposures of others are thus justified. . . .

However, underneath this self-conscious and candid representing that constantly calls attention to its mediations, a real self-execution was secretly taking place. For Dickens had been told by his doctor and many of his friends that he was bringing his illness to a fatal crisis by performing the violent readings from *Oliver Twist.* And yet he willfully continued the performances even though he seems to have believed they would kill him. Concealing this self-executing Dickens is his criminal double, the self-executing Sikes. Far from being a public execution, these readings, which are the representation of a public execution, are also its inversion, the final triumph of the novelistic. No one's death is exposed here. Someone is dying, but only secretly, while the crowd's attention is focused on the duplicitous representation of the death of the double.

Dickens's Odd Use of Christian Themes in *Tale*

Angus Wilson

This excerpt from *The World of Charles Dickens* by novelist and noted literary critic Angus Wilson is a rare example of a modern critical panning of one of Dickens's major works. Although many scholars over the years have objected to specific aspects of *A Tale of Two Cities*, most notably its lack of the usual Dickensian humor, few have faulted the work on so fundamental a basis as Wilson does here. The critic's main objection is what he sees as the author's failure to utilize properly the concept of redemption and other Christian themes that were in vogue in the literary world of Dickens's contemporaries. For instance, Wilson contends that Sydney Carton's famous sacrifice in the finale is an example of pagan rather than Christian heroism because Carton dies for the love of a woman. Wilson also faults *Tale* for what he views as a shallow treatment of the French Revolution.

Oliver Twist has proved to be Dickens's 'pop' novel; *A Tale of Two Cities* has been his great middlebrow success. For theatre-goers of the early twentieth century it was a beloved favourite as [the play] *The Only Way*, with [popular actor] Sir John Martin Harvey as Sydney Carton; at the moment of writing it has reappeared as a musical, which seems likely to take a place in the somewhat old-fashioned repertoires of local amateur operatic societies. I should have liked, simply in order to avoid the charge of artistic snobbery, to number it among his great books; but I cannot do so. It is an important novel in Dickens's canon for two reasons, but neither of them do more than lend it interest irrelevant to artistic success.

The first peculiarity about it is its odd treatment of re-

Excerpted from *The World of Charles Dickens* by Angus Wilson (New York: Viking, 1970). Reproduced by permission of Curtis Brown Ltd., London, on behalf of the Estate of Angus Wilson. Copyright © Angus Wilson, 1970.

nunciation and redemption. In his previous novel [*Little Dorrit*] Dickens had shown how Arthur Clennam had to accept life actively, and even Little Dorrit, the very embodiment of 'blessed are the meek', had to assert herself in order to find herself. Only when they had both accepted happiness and life could they seek salvation away from the world and its noisy, crooked ways. In *A Tale of Two Cities*, however much the nominal hero is Charles Darnay, the real hero is Sydney Carton, the drunken, idling, old-Salopian barrister, and he finds salvation by dying for the happiness of others on the guillotine. The theme of renunciation and redemption continues in the two complete novels Dickens was still to write—Pip must give up the world's goods in *Great Expectations* to redeem his snobbery; so must Bella Wilfer be tried and tried again in *Our Mutual Friend*; and in the same novel idle, cynical Eugene Wrayburn (also a barrister) must come near to death to purify himself for marriage with the heroine, Lizzie Hexam.

Renunciation, redemption, resurrection—we are in these last novels of Dickens well into the world of [Russian novelist Leo] Tolstoy in his late works, or in that of [Russian novelist Fyodor] Dostoevsky's *Crime and Punishment*, or of Dmitri and Ivan Karamazov [characters in Dostoevsky's novel, *The Brothers Karamazov*]. It is essentially a Christian New Testament world, with transcendental overtones. Sydney Carton, who actually gives his life, should surely preach the most Christian of all sermons. And to a degree he does so. As he rides in the tumbril beside the little sempstress she tells him: 'But for you, dear stranger, I should not be so composed . . . nor should I have been able to raise my thoughts to Him [Christ] who was put to death, that we might have hope and comfort here today;' and as the little girl is guillotined and the knitting women count 'Twenty-two', an unembodied voice (is it Sydney Carton or is it the author?) recites: 'I am the Resurrection and the Life, saith the Lord: he that believeth in me, though he were dead, yet he shall live: and whosoever liveth and believeth in me shall never die.' And this Christian note has relevance to the general theme of the book where the two regimes of France—the old order of the Marquis St Evremonde and the new of the revolutionary Defarges—exalt their class, their abstract principles, above the personal ethics of Christianity.

At one point, when the revolutionaries urge Dr Manette to

testify against his own son-in-law as an *aristo* and an *emigré*, Dickens directly points out how the old pagan heroism of sacrificing one's nearest of kin to the good of the republic has been brought hideously alive in French revolutionary zeal. To this extent the book's exaltation of private relationships, private loves (of father for daughter, daughter for father, or of lovers for one another) over abstract principles seems to work with the Christian scheme that Carton's self-sacrifice suggests. And yet . . . in this most seemingly Christian of novels, Dickens's Christian sense seems strangely lacking. Carton's sacrifice is so much a matter of human love that it comes full wheel round to another sort of pagan heroism, not that of the hero who dies for his country, but that of a hero who dies for the sake of love. Christ's death seems only accidental in such a setting; for a Christian reader perhaps the references to Him may seem a little blasphemous. And on the same page, describing Carton's death from which I have quoted the passages about the Crucifixion, Carton and the little sempstress are suddenly called 'these two children of the Universal Mother'. Nevertheless, the novel marks clearly the emphasis on personal relationships as the salvation from the world's evils that was already to be seen in *Little Dorrit* and was to continue in his novels. This in itself makes nonsense of the book's form; for it is intentionally the tale of two cities and above all the tale of a cruel whirlwind that arose and swept through one of them—Paris—in the shape of the Terror.

Sacrificing His Greatest Gifts

Dickens, aware by now of the limitations and needs of weekly serialization, searching (and searching successfully) for a book that would quickly grip his readers' interest, had decided to pare down all in the novel that took away from the action, the events, the rush of the story. To a large extent he was successful. *A Tale of Two Cities* has a minimum of dialogue, subplot, humorous or even melodramatic ornament. It was a sacrifice of all his greatest gifts; and in my opinion it shows that those gifts—of fantastic speech, of animistic description, of deeply absorbed symbolic overtones—are essential to the success of his action. There are splendid scenes, notably Mr Lorry sitting in the quiet, old-fashioned order of Tellson's countinghouse in Paris while the horrors of the September Massacre outside are only suggested in the noises he hears. But the picture of the French Revolution in action (or indeed the cruelties of the nobility that preceded it) seem to me no more than efficient. It is Dickens's revered Carlyle in story form; and Carlyle's *French Revolution* is a good enough story anyway, without fictionalization. Yet it is all there on the pages—Dickens's understanding of the causes of the Revolution, his sympathy with the revolutionaries, his abhorrence of their excesses; but because of its over-simple, active form it becomes a statement and not an evocation. If this were Dickens, he could be counted a proficient master of literature of action to which detail is added without much conviction to give a sense of history. The scenes are greatly inferior to those in *Barnaby Rudge* because the madness which should inform them, which in-

MR. TAPPERTIT IS LOCKED OUT

The absurd characters and humor Wilson admires in Barnaby Rudge and finds lacking in A Tale of Two Cities are illustrated in this charming scene from Rudge, in which the young, conceited but colorful Simon Tappertit, apprentice to the honest old locksmith Mr. Varden, finds himself locked out early one morning and is forced to awaken Mr. Varden's humorless and temperamental servant, Miss Miggs. Hearing a noise from below, she rushes to the window and demands to know who is there.

Mr Tappertit cried "Hush!" and, backing into the road, exhorted her in frenzied pantomime to secrecy and silence.

"Tell me one thing," said Miggs. "Is it thieves?"

"No—no—no!" cried Mr Tappertit.

"Then," said Miggs, more faintly than before, "it's fire. Where is it, sir? It's near this room, I know. I've a good conscience, sir, and would much rather die than go down a ladder. All I wish is, respecting my love to my married sister, Golden Lion Court, number twenty-sivin, second bell-handle on the right-hand door-post."

"Miggs!" cried Mr Tappertit, "don't you know me? Sim, you know—Sim—"

"Oh! what about him!" cried Miggs, clasping her hands. "Is he in any danger? Is he in the midst of flames and blazes? Oh gracious, gracious!"

"Why I'm here, an't I?" rejoined Mr Tappertit, knocking himself on the breast. "Don't you see me? What a fool you are, Miggs!"

deed is Dickens's charge against both the *ancien régime* and the Terror, is quite absent—absent because there is none of the black humour, the wild dialogue, the horrible absurdities of Dennis the hangman, Hugh, Simon Tappertit and Barnaby.

The most telling scenes in *A Tale of Two Cities* are the extremely retired, private scenes in Dr Manette's house in Soho, a house remarkable for its seclusion. The noise of distant feet heard there is used rather heavily by Dickens to warn us of the Revolution to come; but when it comes, it has not the reality of the Soho garden's privacy. Maybe this is a triumph in a book intended to exalt family love, but I doubt if Dickens intended such a kind of triumph—purposefully to fail to bring alive a whole revolution in order to preserve the life of one or two scenes of domestic calm is a modern sort

---

"There!" cried Miggs, unmindful of this compliment. "Why—so it—Goodness, what is the meaning of—If you please, mim, here's—"

"No, no!" cried Mr Tappertit, standing on tiptoe, as if by that means he, in the street, were any nearer being able to stop the mouth of Miggs in the garret. "Don't!—I've been out without leave, and something or another's the matter with the lock. Come down, and undo the shop window, that I may get in that way."

"I dursn't do it, Simmun," cried Miggs—for that was her pronunciation of his Christian name. "I dursn't do it, indeed. You know as well as anybody, how particular I am. And to come down in the dead of night, when the house is wrapped in slumbers and weiled in obscurity." And there she stopped and shivered, for her modesty caught cold at the very thought.

"But Miggs," cried Mr Tappertit, getting under the lamp, that she might see his eyes. "My darling Miggs—"

Miggs screamed slightly.

"—That I love so much, and never can help thinking of,—" and it is impossible to describe the use he made of his eyes when he said this—"do—for my sake, do."

"Oh, Simmun," cried Miggs, "that is worse than all. I know if I come down, you'll go, and—"

"And what, my precious?" said Mr Tappertit.

"And try," said Miggs, hysterically, "to kiss me, or some such dreadfulness; I know you will!"

"I swear I won't," said Mr Tappertit, with remarkable earnestness. "Upon my soul I won't."

of complexity alien from his genius. The truth is, I think, that for all the two cartloads of reference books from the London Library, which Carlyle sent round to him to help him prepare the novel, the French Revolution remained unrealized in Dickens's book. Private renunciation and private love are the real themes of a novel which ostensibly treats of the greatest public event of his era.

Ultimate Justice over Injustice in *A Tale of Two Cities*

John R. Reed

In this excerpt from his book *Dickens and Thackeray: Punishment and Forgiveness*, distinguished scholar and professor of English at Wayne State University John R. Reed addresses the themes of justice and injustice in *A Tale of Two Cities*. According to Reed, the novel rarely mentions forgiveness or mercy and focuses instead on the consequences of injustice, especially in relation to the workings of fate and destiny. For example, Reed states that because the French aristocracy has institutionalized injustice it is destined to pay a heavy price, both on earth and in the afterlife. "An unjust ruling class will inevitably suffer punishment for its conduct," writes Reed; at the same time, those who commit crimes in the name of revolutionary justice will be punished, for "retribution comes to all who transgress." Thus, Reed concludes, Dickens believed in a universe overseen by providence or otherwise endowed with the quality of ultimate justice.

Something is very wrong with justice in *A Tale of Two Cities* (1859). Both English and French legal systems seem more capable of persecuting the innocent than prosecuting the guilty. An outlaw like Jerry Cruncher may voice disgust at the inhuman legal punishment of quartering, but only from self-interest. And when the mob overthrows corrupt authority in France, it imposes a mirror injustice, replacing one bloodthirstiness with another. The narrator specifically describes the self-appointed Tribunal as "unjust." Many crimes in this book are punished, but not through official channels. This is true in much of Dickens' fiction, where public institutions rarely succeed in being just. Dickens wants a regime that combines a sense of justice with a sense of mercy, but under these requirements it is difficult to assign authority to punish. Christ recommended forgiving of offenders and advised turning the other cheek. Thus individual Christians must not exact justice. But if the unfeeling, mechanical, even corrupt state is unqualified to dispense justice, who has the moral right and the power and means to do so?

Like [his friend, historian Thomas] Carlyle ... Dickens assumed that true justice is administered finally by providence. That does not mean that most offenses are not punished through human agency, but that the guiding power for such justice is divine. Human beings generate their deserts through their conduct and, in that sense, all punishments are self-begotten. Most of Dickens' novels focus on punishing offenses or patterns of offense in specific institutions or individuals. But *A Tale of Two Cities* emphasizes the fates of nations rather than of individuals. Because history does not forgive, there is very little discussion of forgiveness, or even pardon or mercy, in this novel, which is overwhelmingly occupied with illustrating the consequences of unwise, unjust, and inhuman behavior.

FATE AND SECRET MEMORIES

Perhaps to convey a greater sense of the tragic dimensions of the French Revolution, the novel says little about providence, but a good deal about fate and destiny. At the outset of *A Tale of Two Cities* the narrator remarks that many years before the Revolution, Fate had already marked the trees that would be used to construct the guillotine. Madame Defarge, knitting the names of those who are to be consigned to death when the Revolution begins, works "with the steadfastness of Fate," suggesting an analogy with the Greek fates who spun, measured, and cut the threads of human life. Learning that Darnay/St. Evrémonde has married Lucie Manette in England, Defarge hopes that for Lucie's sake "Destiny will keep her husband out of France."

This concern for the determining power of fate is reflected in the narrator's manner, for he regularly offers confident forecasts of what is to come. Partly this is because he is telling a story whose end—the French Revolution—is in the past and thus already known to his audience. There can be no suspense about the outcome of public events. But the narrator's many proleptic passages also confirm the rigidity of the events being related. Repetition of the motif clusters of wine/blood/stain and of hastening footsteps gathering into a crowd, along with direct forecasts by the narrator ("The time was to come, when that wine [blood] too would be spilled on the street stones, and when the stain of it would be red upon many there"), enhance the foreknown events in an operatic manner, like the . . . value-laden motifs that accompany and foreshadow events in [German composer Richard] Wagner's operas.

But if these and other direct forecasts of what is to come suggest a known, predictable world, a second powerful tendency of the narrative is to insist upon the mystery that is within us. Despite the many indications that life is plotted by fate, in fact not all of these signs are accurate or trustworthy. Madame Defarge does not control the destinies of others, but is herself only part of a larger force. Madame Defarge points her finger "as if it were the finger of Fate" at Lucie's child, but the implied doom never comes to pass. The resurrection theme in the novel is intimately related to its "psychological" kernel, but it is also linked by its overt Christian association with the idea of forgiveness and redemption. Human sympathy is the amulet by which the charmed doors of the mind and heart can be reopened. When Lucie first succeeds in penetrating the muddle of her father's mind to touch his heart, he sobs tempestuously then yields "to the calm that must follow all storms—emblem to humanity, of the rest and silence into which the storm called Life must hush at last." Dr. Manette is himself emblematic of the mystery that all humans are to one another. In his confused state following his release after more than seventeen years of imprisonment, "No human intelligence could read the mysteries of his mind in the scared blank wonder of his face.". . .

In *A Tale of Two Cities*, personal and public secrets are intertwined and mysteries of the human heart are played out in public venues. In this novel as in others, secrecy is associated with suffering, death, and burial. But just as Dr. Manette, in being recalled to life from his "burial" in prison, becomes the embodied expression of a long-kept secret, so a major theme of the novel is that one way to counteract the power of death is through bringing to light the secrets within us, rooted as they are in suffering. This theme is related to Dickens' broader view that we must treasure memory—both good and bad—because out of memories come our resources for encountering the difficult experiences of life. In *A Tale of Two Cities*, secret memories are both private and communal. The communal "secrets" are already known to the reader because they are part of historical record, but the private secrets remain a mystery until the narrative exposes them to light. Thus, while the public narrative moves unswervingly toward its foreknown denoument, an accompanying narrative line presents a sequence of secrets gradually exposed to reveal the dark and bright elements harbored within human nature.

HATRED ANSWERS HATRED

Mr. Lorry's suggestion to Dr. Manette that he might be able to defend himself against relapses in his mental health by sharing his secret with someone else is a straightforward version of Dickens' belief that the secrets of the heart may become useful when faced and shared. That which is repressed, that from which we unconsciously avert our gaze, only increases its power by being ignored. This is true in the history of nations as well as of individuals. The narrative, by temporally dislocating the order of its revelations, subtly indicates how complicated and insidious the perpetuation of evil can be, through the failure to face the secrets of the past. When Charles Darnay is arrested and "buried," "in secret," he both duplicates and anticipates Dr. Manette's history. ... Only after Charles' incarceration do we learn the details of Dr. Manette's unjust confinement by the St. Evrémonde brothers. Charles' imprisonment is a foreshadowing of the secret we will soon learn. . . . The two imprisonments are intimately linked. Dr. Manette recovers his full capacities in working to free his son-in-law. "For the first time the Doctor felt, now, that his suffering was strength and power." His suffering having been made public, he is endowed with a productive strength that repression could never produce. Ironically, Dr. Manette is actually operating against his own scripting of history, but that revelation has yet to be made. At this point, what is important is the suggestion that torment can be transformed into triumph and that pain may be the agent of beneficial transformation.

The disclosure of our secrets is not always safe or constructive. The secret that the Doctor has himself deeply repressed comes to light and recondemns Charles to death. In the depths of his agony, Dr. Manette put in writing his curse on the whole St. Evrémonde family and now that curse has its effect. Like a prescripted fate, Dr. Manette's version of history now becomes the official text that the revolutionaries are determined to play out. Nested in this lesson on repression and revelation, suffering and salvation, is an even more basic moral ground. Hatred, rage, and vindictiveness are not the emotions that will improve human conditions. When hatred answers hatred, only more evil will be propagated in the world. Dr. Manette's cry for universal revenge against the entire family of his oppressors is as unjust as their behavior, and predictably begets additional suffering upon the victim who has become transgressor in his turn. In this way it reflects at the personal level what occurs at the public level with the violence of the revolutionaries. There are good and bad secrets in our hearts and we must learn to understand them ourselves and face them. Lucie's heart is "a mystery" to Dr. Manette, but it is clear to everyone that it is a benign mystery. So certain is Carton of the benignity of that heart that he wants "the last confidence of [his] life" to repose in Lucie's "pure and innocent breast" to be shared by no one else. This is the holy secret of another being's unselfish love. Moreover, it is this love for Lucie that prompts Carton to look into "the mystery of [his] own wretched heart," and by facing its darknesses wrest from them a final shining victory.

Madame Defarge is the focus of error in *A Tale of Two Cities*, embodying the worst of human impulses and turning even apparent virtues into crimes. She is contrasted particularly with the Manettes, but with Darnay as well. If Madame Defarge's threads represent a terrible future, worked to its design out of the past and present, Lucie is herself "the golden thread" that unites her father's past and present over the gulf of his suppressed misery. And just as Lucie is the constructive force whose secret is a loving heart, so the secret in Madame Defarge's heart is an unforgiving hatred and a claim for revenge against all of the St. Evrémonde family. Dr. Manette has excluded Charles from his enmity—a form of forgiveness—but Madame Defarge has brooded on her injury until it has become a need for personal retribution. Her secret, saved until the last moment, is that the peasant family devastated by the St. Evrémonde brothers' cruelty was her family. As long as Madame Defarge labors for the oppressed she is triumphant and safe, but the moment she takes justice into her own hands she puts herself at risk, and in trying to injure Lucie and her daughter she destroys herself with her own weapon. . . .

AS ONE SOWS, SO MUST ONE REAP

A Tale of Two Cities is, then, a history of individual secrets and their disclosures in the context of the permanent mystery of the human heart, but it is also a history of two nations in a specific period of chronological time. In this history, as I have already noted, there are no secrets because the major events are foreknown. Yet this larger movement of the story is intimately related to the movement of individual careers.

The greatest historical guilt rests with the French aristocracy. The most obvious thing about them in this novel is that they are self-indulgent, arrogant, exploitive, and unjust. They cringe before their superiors and lord it over their inferiors. At the Monseigneur's reception in Paris there is an elegant turnout of court hangers-on. The narrator observes "that all the company at the grand hotel of Monseigneur were perfectly dressed. If the Day of Judgment had only been ascertained to be a dress day, everybody there would have been eternally correct." But the whole point about Judgment Day is that all external ornament, all disguise, will be put aside and each individual will answer for his or her behavior. For most individuals some mercy will be required, since we are all fallible and likely to have some maculations to be forgiven and expunged. But the French aristocracy of *A Tale of Two Cities* has, as a class, institutionalized injustice and will have a heavy debt of guilt to pay. The narrator provides a sample of this behavior in the Marquis St. Evrémonde as he leaves the Monseigneur's party in a foul mood. The marquis urges his coachman to make speed, and, as a consequence, the coach runs down a child in the street. The marquis reprimands the poor people in the street for not being able to tend their children and is more worried about his horses than about the child. He throws the child's distraught parent a coin as a compensation for his loss. This callous behavior is emblematic because it manifests two central abominations in Dickens' moral economy—violation of family feeling, especially when focused upon a child, and the transformation of human values into monetary terms. When he arrives back at his estate the marquis is equally callous and arrogant toward his own tenants. He refuses to provide a simple marker for the grave of a woman's dead husband.

The marquis' actions offer representative and concrete examples of abuses by the French aristocracy. They are narrated in a manner calculated to excite common human sympathies, the narrator's method of weighting his plot toward retribution. But the accumulating burden of guilt is historical, not merely national. France may be a hell of injustice and cruelty but England is not much better. "In England," the narrator remarks, "there was scarcely an amount of order and protection to justify much national boasting.". . .

And yet putting to death does not clear away the midden of accumulating social guilt. Putting to death is a public way of trying to forget. With the offender dead and buried, one may forget the occasion of the crime. . . . A social evil may be repressed and forgotten, but as with the psychological operation of individuals, it will eventually find release and express itself all the more forcefully for having been so long held back. The murder of the marquis is an individual event, but again symptomatic of what awaits his class when the hidden rage of the populace breaks into the open. Madame Defarge understands when she declares, "Vengeance and retribution require a long time; it is the rule.". . .

Madame Defarge alludes to the moral rule that evil brings its own consequences, a rule that was for Dickens a natural process as well. Thus the narrator uses images of such natural forces as storms and rising seas to describe the approach of the Revolution. As one sows so must one reap, the narrator suggests, elaborating the maxim when he explains that French aristocracy and British orthodoxy alike talk of "this terrible Revolution as if it were the one only harvest ever known under the skies that had not been sown—as if nothing had ever been done, or omitted to be done, that had led to it—as if observers of the wretched millions in France, and of the misused and perverted resources that should have made them prosperous had not seen it inevitably coming, years before, and had not in plain words recorded what they saw."

A CONTINUING WEB OF VIOLENCE

And so the Revolution occurs. Secret hatred breaks into sight, becoming a kind of madness. The woman known as Vengeance typifies the unthinking violence of those who have broken from their repression with no constructive plan. They can only glory in the destruction of a power that once kept them "underground." Violent response to injustice, however, is not the answer. . . . If it is not possible to pardon the outrages of the past, an individual or a people must not commit the equal error of perpetuating similar outrages in the present. The links or threads of act and consequence will in this case only fashion a continuing web of violence and retribution. Set against such a determinant sequence is the golden thread of love, forgiveness, and mercy embodied in Lucie Manette.

The connection between national and individual repression is focused in the St. Evrémondes' case. They rape a peasant girl and murder her brother. The St. Evrémonde brothers are humiliated not by the dastardly nature of these intimate crimes, but because the peasant boy dared to struggle against his oppressors on equal terms. It is to keep this embarrassing information secret that the aristocrats have Manette abducted and "buried alive." As witness to the truth, he becomes the memory they want suppressed, the secret they want hidden. . . .

Madame Defarge is the sister of the raped girl and murdered boy. Her whole involvement in the revolutionary cause has been fueled less by an abstract desire for justice and social progress than by a secret personal hatred, a craving toward private revenge. Madame Defarge is the reverse image of Darnay, just as she is of Lucie. Seeking to be just and to expunge the guilt of his class, Darnay is unaware of his own intimate involvement in a central, representative crime. By contrast, Madame Defarge's apparent concern for her class masks a private vendetta spurring her to public action. Ironically Madame Defarge, who has labored at bringing a specific destiny into being, dies "accidentally" by her own weapon when she struggles with Miss Pross in an effort to get at Lucie and her child. Dickens was fully conscious of the implicit moral balance he wished to achieve by this outcome; defending the use of accident in fiction generally, and specifically in the scene of Madame Defarge's death. "Where the accident is inseparable from the passion and action of the character; where it is strictly consistent with the entire design, and arises out of some culminating proceeding on the part of the individual which the whole story has led up to; it seems to me to become, as it were, an act of divine justice." Dickens adds that he purposely used the "half-comic intervention" of Miss Pross to emphasize the angry woman's failure and to contrast her mean death to a desperate but bold death in the streets. Madame Defarge's "mean death" is also opposed "to the dignity of Carton's.". . .

BREAKING THE CHAIN OF CRIME AND REVENGE

By incorporating fictional private histories, containing secrets to be disclosed through the narrative's progress within the larger historical, and thus known, story of the French Revolution—which contains no secrets about its development—the narrator can establish a tension between two ways of viewing justice in the universe in a manner that resembles the narrative strategy of *Bleak House*, where the more personal and private outlook is chiefly provided by Esther and the general and social by the third-person narrator. The great events that we describe as historical are governed by providence, or by fate, in the sense that implies inevitability. An unjust ruling class will inevitably suffer punishment for its conduct. At the personal level individuals are free to make crucial moral decisions that might bind them to or free them from "destiny," which is to say the evil consequences of bad acts. By choosing pardon, mercy, or forgiveness, individuals can break the chain of crime and revenge that leads to greater and greater suffering. If the grindstone is a symbol of the unthinking viciousness of rebellion, the guillotine is a symbol of its false justice. But even that symbol can be transformed. The positive power to transform symbols is at the heart of Sydney Carton's crowning act. Like all thoughtful human beings, Carton is something of a mystery to himself, and certainly he is a mystery to others, who cannot understand the waste he has made of his life. Carton is as he is partly because he can establish no clear identity for himself. He sinks his own identity into Stryver's work. He casually saves Darnay's life by calling attention to their apparent interchangeability. The one way he has of anchoring his nature is by the secret buried alive in his heart—his love for Lucie. But this, too, he shares with Darnay. Carton represents lack of initiative, whereas Darnay is all conscientious effort. But in the most dissipated among us, if only they have faith in some enduring belief or feeling, the power of transformation, or resurrection, as the language of the novel would have it, remains. He can *become* Charles Darnay. . . .
By assuming Darnay's identity while retaining his own char-

acter, Carton divests himself of his worst self. His private secret of love for Lucie becomes the public secret of his disguise. The mystery of his nature becomes the sacrament of
his act. As he mounts to the guillotine, this symbol of dreadful rage and revenge is transformed to a symbol of love. By
Carton's act it comes to resemble Christ's cross; his death is
an atonement reflecting the great Atonement that makes existence possible in a world complicated by evil destinies.
Carton's act involves not only self-forgiveness but forgiveness for the violence that men do to one another. The great
public crime of the Terror begets the great private sacrifice
and redemption betokening love. . . .

ONLY THE FOOLISH WISH TO FORGET

Another interesting feature of this novel emphasizes the role
of analogous narratives embedded within the larger narrative. The narrator's task is to indicate the differences between historical and personal "fates," and to suggest how experience may be read to reveal the secrets of human destiny
and to therefore change that destiny for the better. One way
for the narrator to educate his characters and readers is to
indicate by way of embedded narratives what might be expected in the main narrative, as Christ's parables illustrate
his larger message. When Mr. Lorry meets Lucie at Dover to
escort her to France, he tells her "the story of one of our cus-
tomers." This is an account of her unnamed father's circumstances, designed to prepare her for the revelation that
he is alive. Dickens and other Victorian novelists frequently
used this and similar devices, having characters break good
or bad news gradually to their audiences, and so such an instance is not remarkable. Later an analogous tale prepares
the reader for events to come in the same way that Lorry has
prepared Lucie, though not so openly. Darnay recounts an
anecdote about a prisoner in the Tower of London who had
hidden a document in his cell that was later unearthed. Dr.
Manette's response, and other clues, suggest that Dr.
Manette knows of a similar case. Of course Darnay's anecdote, which does not mention the contents of the recovered
documents, foreshadows Dr. Manette's hidden account, recovered by Defarge, describing the primal transgression that
generates all of the events that follow. Dr. Manette's narrative is itself an analogue of the larger history of France—the
suppression ("burying") of truth by the aristocracy to ensure

the continuance of its own privileges. . . .

These narratives within the narrative and other anticipatory methods, such as the reiterated theme of approaching footsteps, create a predictive, proleptic effect very like that of statements in which the narrator openly anticipates the future. Such proleptic references seem to endorse a world of inevitable unfoldings where what will be is already existent, as though the future were foreknown and therefore already history. But these various forms of foreshadowing are transformed into a positive rather than pessimistically determinist version of anticipation when, at the conclusion of the novel, the narrator relates what Sydney Carton's words on his way to execution would have been ("and they were prophetic") if he had uttered them. Carton's conjectured story tells what the future will bring both for the individuals he loves and for England and France. The narrative that Carton projects into the future ends with Lucie's son telling Carton's story to his son. So the narrative we have just read becomes, at its conclusion, a story of a time gone by but made ever present by retelling, just as Carton's life, at the moment it ends, becomes an exemplary story worthy of being repeated. Moreover, both Carton's story and Dickens' novel count on the instructive redundancy of frequent repetition to make memorable the errors of the past and the virtues of those who struggled against them. In letting Carton tell the story of the beneficent future, the narrator endorses his own task, for his novel is the calling to life of a communal memory, and its account of individuals who suffered intensely is designed to touch the heart and make it alive to injustice in its own day, much in the way the Christmas ghosts [in Dickens's *A Christmas Carol*] use the past and the future to revive Scrooge's heart. Only the wicked or foolish wish to forget. . . . Unresolved suffering or injustice must be recalled, faced, and transformed into strength in nations as in individual human beings. Narratives can help us to do this; they can capture in a memorable form the moral energies that help us to understand the secrets of the human heart, and those great rules by which Dickens believed mankind was governed, rules ensuring that, in time, retribution comes to all who transgress and victory to all who suffer. This was Dickens' great hope and the moral foundation for the stories he told.

CHAPTER 2

Pivotal Characters in *A Tale of Two Cities*

READINGS ON
A TALE OF TWO CITIES

Dickens's Characters Are Fantasy Versions of Real People

Leonard Manheim

In the following essay, literary scholar Leonard Manheim explains that Dickens based some of the main characters in *A Tale of Two Cities* on real people, including himself. For example, Manheim maintains that Lucie's character represents the actress Ellen Ternan, some twenty-seven years younger than Dickens, with whom he fell in love and may have had an affair in the 1850s. In particular, says Manheim, Dickens employed the technique of "multiple projection," or transforming a real person's character into two or more fictional characters. The most obvious example is that of Sydney Carton and Charles Darnay, who represent two sides of a fantasy hero patterned after Dickens himself. According to Manheim, Carton, standing for Dickens's dark and sinful side, must die, not only for his own sins, but also for those of Dickens, including the author's adulterous longings for Ellen Ternan. Manheim also discusses multiple versions of the father figure in the novel.

Dickens scholars have never been able to forgive *A Tale of Two Cities* its popularity—its very special kind of popularity. *Pickwick Papers* has survived the adulation of the special Pickwick cult; *David Copperfield* has survived the sentimental biography-hunting of the Dickensians; even *Great Expectations* may survive its selection as the Dickens work to be presented in "service courses" on the lower college level. But *A Tale of Two Cities* will never wholly live down the fact that it has received a kiss of death by its almost universal adoption as the Dickens work to be presented to secondary school students, usually during the tenth year of their formal edu-

Excerpted from "A Tale of Two Characters: A Study in Multiple Projection" by Leonard Manheim, *Dickens Studies Annual*, vol. 1 (1970), pp. 225-37. Reprinted by permission of AMS Press, New York, N.Y.

cation. Several factors have contributed to the persistence of the high-school syllabus-makers in prescribing the reading of *A Tale of Two Cities*. The first reason seems to be its compactness; it is not as long as most other Dickens works. In my own experience, it has been preferred even when *David Copperfield* was permitted as an alternative, purely because *David Copperfield* was so much longer. A second reason, which stems from the era when all novels were suspect, is the fact that *A Tale of Two Cities* is an historical novel, and the curse was considered removed from the "novel" because of the "history." But the factor which probably loomed largest in the minds of the syllabus-makers was the "purity" of *A Tale of Two Cities*. It is wholly without the taint of immorality; it seems to be practically free of sexuality. (Can the account of the rape of Madame Defarge's sister in Doctor Manette's secret narrative be called sexuality? It is easy enough to pass over it—it is so hazily referred to; and in any event, it is a story of an occurrence in a benighted foreign country and hence a horrible example of "foreign" morality.) . . . I submit that the criterion for high school reading is usually—or at any rate used to be—one of superficial absence of any "immoral" element. Yet it is ironically noteworthy that *A Tale of Two Cities*, on a less superficial level, is the product of a great sexual crisis in the author's life, an upheaval in his psychosexual pattern which has been but dimly comprehended. Perhaps it would be as well to recount once again the facts as they have been clarified by recent scholarship.

DICKENS THE ACTOR

On 10 February, in 1851, Dickens wrote to Wills, his long-suffering editorial assistant on *Household Words*, asking Wills to play the part of a servant in the comedy *Not So Bad as We Seem*, a typical nineteenth-century play written by the prolific Bulwer Lytton for production by Dickens' semi-permanent company of amateur actors. Dickens hastened to assure Wills that he would be in good company—among talented literary amateur actors. . . . The over-burdened Wills found it impossible to add participation in his principal's theatrical ventures to his other duties, and he politely declined the offer. A little while later, Dickens wrote to his friend Augustus Egg, scenic designer of many of the productions, asking him if he could induce Wilkie Collins to accept the role. Collins did accept and thus began the friendship with Dickens which was to last until the latter's death. There was nearly fifteen years' difference in age between the two; their temperaments were fundamentally dissimilar; yet the influence of Collins on every phase of the latter years of Dickens' life and work is most marked, and there was ample indication that he tended, as time went on, to usurp the confidential position formerly held exclusively by John Forster, to the no small annoyance of that worthy gentleman.

In Collins, Dickens found an admirable traveling companion, one who introduced him to phases of life at home and abroad with which he had formerly been familiar by hearsay only, one who was reasonably free from Victorian prejudices so dear to the heart of John Forster. In Collins he found an equally enthusiastic devotee of the theatre, a competent and thorough deviser of complex plots (frequently of a most melodramatic character). It was Collins who put together the melodrama *The Lighthouse*, with a highly emotional leading role which Dickens delighted to play. It was he who was entrusted with the task of dramatizing the very worst of the Dickens Christmas numbers, *No Thoroughfare*, for professional production; and it was he who concocted *The Frozen Deep*, that queer melodrama in which Dickens played his last performance on the amateur stage. . . .

Much of the idea of *The Frozen Deep* seems to have originated with Dickens himself rather than with Collins. It was Dickens who inserted the "comedy relief," Dickens who wrote the verse prologue which Forster spoke from behind the curtain before the opening, closing with these words:

> But, that the secrets of the vast Profound
> Within us, an exploring hand may sound,
> Testing the region of the ice-bound soul,
> Seeking the passage at its northern pole,
> Soft'ning the horrors of its wintry sleep,
> Melting the surface of that "Frozen Deep."

The plot of the play whose hero Dickens so greatly longed to "embody in his own person" is worthy of being examined closely, when we consider how much it meant to him during his composition of *A Tale of Two Cities* and how clearly it constituted a turning point in his life.

> The first act makes us acquainted with four young ladies living in Devon, each of whom has a lover serving with a Polar expedition. Clara Burnham not only has her betrothed out in the icy regions, but the rejected lover who was sworn to kill

him wherever and whenever they meet, though he does not even know the name of his rival. Clara, haunted by the fear that some mysterious influence may reveal them to each other, tells her story to Lucy Crayford. As she does so, a crimson sunset dies away to grey and Nurse Esther goes about the house murmuring of scenes that come to her from "the land o' ice and snaw." She stands, as night falls, by the misty blue of the window, describing to the young ladies her bloody vision from the Northern seas. Lucy Crayford shudders and calls for lights: Clara Burnham swoons.

The second act is set in the arctic regions. The stranded men are in a hut deciding who is to go and seek relief. Frank Aldersley is chosen by lot, and when somebody else falls out, Richard Wardour has to accompany him. Just before they start Wardour discovers that Aldersley is his hated rival.

The third act takes place in a cavern in Newfoundland. The girls, smartly dressed in crinolines, their Scotch nurse, and some members of the expedition are present, but neither Wardour nor Aldersley. Presently a ragged maniac rushes in and is given food and drink. He has escaped from an ice-floe but is not too demented to recognise and be recognised by Clara Burnham, who suspects him of having murdered her Frank. As soon as he understands this he goes off, returning a few minutes later with Aldersley in his arms to lay at Clara's feet. "Often," he gasps, "in supporting Aldersley through snow-drifts and on ice-floes have I been tempted to leave him sleeping!" He has not done so and is now exhausted to death.

Dickens played Wardour; and Collins, Aldersley. Purposely for the "part," each of them grew a substantial beard which he kept in later life. During the early private showings and at the special performance for the Queen, the women's roles were played by lady amateurs. However, when it was decided to repeat the play at Manchester for the benefit of the late Douglass Jerrold's family, it became apparent that the size of the house (it held three thousand spectators at one performance) would require the engagement of professionals for the women's roles. It was on the recommendation of a friendly theatrical manager that Mrs. Ternan and her two daughters, Maria and Ellen, were engaged for the production. Mrs. Ternan played the Scottish nurse; Maria Ternan played the leading role of Clara Burnham; and Ellen played one of the other girls, probably Lucy. ... It was during the brief period of rehearsals at Tavistock House, with Maria and Ellen rushing in and out of his study, Ellen perching on the arm of his chair and turning soulful eyes upon him as he instructed her in the interpretation of her role, that young love began to spring anew in the breast of the forty-five-year-old author. Collins was enthralled by Dickens' brilliance during the Manchester performances. "Dickens," he wrote, "surpassed himself. He literally electrified the audience.". . .

Aghast for a moment after the first emotional shock had passed, Dickens tried to run away from himself again, this time with Collins. The trip is the one described in their joint literary effort known as *The Lazy Tour of Two Idle Apprentices*. When it was over, the problem was solved and Dickens had cast Victorian morality to the winds and was an ardent suitor for the favors of the young lady. . . .

JEKYLL AND HYDE

It was in such troubled days that *A Tale of Two Cities* was conceived and, for the most part, written. It was the work used to launch the new publication *All the Year Round*, which succeeded *Household Words* after Dickens' break with his former publishers, occasioned by his frantic desire to suppress the Ternan scandal. The whole work is impregnated with the spirit of the theatre. . . . The work has a complicated plot-structure which yet stands up better under analysis than any novel since *Barnaby Rudge*, with which it at once compels comparison. Like that former work, it is markedly deficient in humor. There seems to be no room in it for both the old comedy and also the new Collins-inspired melodrama. There is not even as much comedy in the new work as in *Barnaby Rudge*, the former novel of revolutionary days, for Miss Pross and Jerry Cruncher [the mild comic relief in *A Tale of Two Cities*] cannot bear even so much of the burden as was formerly shared by Miss Miggs and Sim Tappertit [the comic relief in *Barnaby Rudge*].

The compulsive quality of the writing of *A Tale of Two Cities* is revealed in the preface [of the novel]. Whenever we find an author stressing such compulsions, we can safely conclude that we are dealing with "repressed" inspiration from unconscious sources. The most striking effect upon the novel of the emotionally disturbed period which produced it lies in the Dr. Jekyll–Mr. Hyde aspect of its leading male character. The word "character" is used in the singular intentionally, for in *A Tale of Two Cities* Dickens developed even more fully than was usual for him the tendency to embody his own ideal of himself, his own Fantasy-Hero in two or more characters (*multiple projection*). Charles Darnay and Sydney Carton are two plainly delineated faces of the same coin. Their names are extensions of a familiar pattern. The fortunate-unfortunate French nobleman bears his author's Christian name with a surname which uses the first initial of *Dickens* to bear out the fantasy of noble birth in disguise, since Charles is said to have assumed the name Darnay upon dropping the hated appellation Evrémonde, adapting his new surname from his mother's noble name of D'Aulnay, eliding the aristocratic *de* in deference to British taste. In the name Sydney Carton the trend is more hidden; yet it too is a simple cipher, easily susceptible of solution— as it is meant to be. The *Charles* element is transferred to the *Car-* syllable of the last name; in the first syllable of *Sidney*, we have the same softening of *Dick-* which may be noticed in the name *Jarndyce* (pronounced Jahn-diss) in *Bleak House*, here reversed (another reversal) to form Syd. The implication is apparent. Both Carton and Darnay are Dickens (not literally, of course, but in fantasy); the point is further stressed by the fortuitous fact that they look alike.

Consider this last point for a moment. Carton, during Darnay's English trial for treason, points out the resemblance between himself and Darnay to his senior counsel, Mr. Stryver, who uses it (so it is said) to discredit the testimony of a witness, a witness who had testified that he had seen the defendant Darnay descend by stealth from the Dover mail in order to spy upon a garrison and dockyard, admitting that he had never seen the accused upon any other occasion.

> "You say again you are quite sure that it *was* the prisoner?" The witness was quite sure.
> "Did you ever see anybody very like the prisoner?" Not so like (the witness said), as that he could be mistaken.
> "Look well upon that gentleman, my learned friend there," pointing to him who had tossed the paper over, "and then look well upon the prisoner. How say you? Are they very like each other?"
> Allowing for my learned friend's appearance being careless and slovenly, if not debauched, they were sufficiently like each other to surprise, not only the witness, but everybody present, when they were thus brought into comparison. My Lord being prayed to bid my learned friend lay aside his wig, and giving no very gracious consent, the likeness became much more remarkable. My Lord inquired of Mr. Stryver, (the prisoner's counsel), whether they were next to try Mr. Carton (name of my learned friend) for treason? But

Mr. Stryver replied to my Lord, no; but he would ask the witness to tell him whether what happened once, might happen twice; whether he would have been so confident, having seen it; and more. The upshot of which was, to smash this witness like a crockery vessel, and shiver his part of the case to useless lumber (II, 3)

Now any competent trial lawyer will recognize that this is very bad cross-examination. The fact that Mr. Darnay resembled Mr. Carton does not really impeach the credibility of the witness' testimony, unless, as the presiding judge suggested, it had been counsel's intention to show that Mr. Carton was also in the neighborhood at the time. An identification by a witness may be impeached far better by his inability to pick the prisoner out of a group of people (a "line-up," for example) who do not in any way resemble one another. Yet for Dickens it fits into a set pattern. Darnay is first accused of treason in England (treachery, betrayal of his country, let it be remembered—parallel in fantasy-life to a man's "betrayal" of his wife). He is saved by his *alter ego*, Carton. Seventeen years later the accusation of betrayal is renewed before another, "foreign" tribunal—foreign both geographically and in the standard of loyalty which it imposes. Now Carton is impotent. He cannot plead in the new court. He cannot answer the fatal and misguided denunciation of the destructive father-image, the Law. But he can assume the place of his double and die in his stead, making a propitiatory sacrifice of himself by which he clears and saves the innocent person of the favored hero. Never was there a more felicitously contrived scapegoat pattern.

All of the virtue which would make the favored lover worthy of his virgin is embodied in Jekyll-Darnay. All of the vice—gloomy, Byronic, objectively unmotivated and unexplained—is concentrated in Hyde-Carton (who, of course, never gets the girl), for whom it is purged away by his "full, perfect, and sufficient sacrifice," not for the sins of the whole world to be sure, but for the sinful love of one Charles Dickens for one Ellen Ternan. Even the self-satisfying sense of resurrection, an "undying" after death, is accomplished by the final picture of Sydney's mind just before the guillotine falls, envisaging the rosy future which is to follow for all concerned, even his own rebirth in his child-namesake. How can Ellen hesitate now? Her middle-aged lover is not only the most fascinating of men; he is also (by a vicarious propitiatory sacrifice) the most guiltless, and she will share that pristine state of innocence with him forever!

THE DREAM VIRGIN

Lucie is basically only one more in the line of Dickensian virgin-heroines whom the critic Edwin Pugh felicitously called "feminanities." Yet, as Professor Edgar Johnson clearly saw, there was a subtle distinction.

> Lucie . . . is given hardly any individual traits at all, although her appearance, as Dickens describes it, is like that of Ellen, "a short, slight, pretty figure, a quantity of golden hair, a pair of blue eyes," and it may be that her one unique physical characteristic was drawn from Ellen too: "a forehead with a singular capacity (remembering how young and smooth it was), of lifting and knitting itself into an expression that was not quite one of perplexity, or wonder, or alarm, though it included all the four expressions.". . . The fact that Lucie and Dr. Manette at the time of his release from the Bastille are of almost the same age as Ellen and Dickens does not mean that the Doctor's feeling for his daughter is the emotion Dickens felt for the pretty, blue-eyed actress, although the two merge perhaps in his fervent declaration [in his letter protesting the scandal, a letter which he "never meant to be published"] that he knows Ellen to be as "innocent and pure, and as good as my own dear daughter."

But Lucie fails to fit into the pattern of the unattainable dream-virgin of the earlier novels in at least one other respect. Most of Dickens' earlier heroine-ideals do not marry until the last-chapter summation of the "lived-happily-ever-after" pattern. Lucie is married, happily married, through much of the book. She maintains a household for her husband and her father, and she finds room for compassion, if not love, for the erring Carton. What is more, she has children, two of them. Yet she seems never to grow older. She was seventeen in 1775; she is, to all intents and purposes, seventeen in 1792. In the interim she has allegedly given birth to two Dickens-ideal infants, two of the most sickening little poppets we could possibly expect from one who, despite his experience as the father of ten children, still sought desperately to re-create infancy and childhood in an image which would affirm his own concept of unworldly innocence. Let the reader take a firm grip on himself and read the dying words of the little son of Charles and Lucie Darnay, who died in early childhood for no other reason, it must seem, than to give the author another opportunity to wallow in bathos.

"Dear papa and mamma, I am very sorry to leave you both, and to leave my pretty sister; but I am called, and I must go!"

. . . .

"Poor Carton! Kiss him for me!" (II, 21)

Poor Carton, indeed! Poor Dickens! Little Lucie is not much better, for in Paris, after her father's condemnation, when her mother is mercifully unconscious and unaware of Carton's presence, she cries out in sweet childish innocence to friend Sydney:

> "Oh, Carton, Carton, dear Carton!... Now that you have come, I think you will do something to help mamma, something to save papa! Oh, look at her, dear Carton! Can you, of all the people who love her bear to see her so?" (III, 11)

Out of the mouths of babes! At this point there is obviously nothing for Sydney to do but head straight for the nearest guillotine.

But Sydney is not to be left wholly without his own dream girl. Just as the purified Darnay is permitted to live out his life with the "attained" (and untainted) Lucie, so the dying Carton is accompanied to his execution by the virgin-victim, the innocent seamstress whom he solaces and strengthens until the final moments of their love-death, although her first glance had revealed that he was not the man Darnay whom she had previously admired....

MULTIPLE FATHERS

There is no lack of father-counterparts [multiple projections of the father figure, a potent image to Dickens], for the law-as-father has become blended with the fear of condemnation by society, which thereby also becomes a symbolic father figure. Society and its moral sanctions constitute the only fly in the ointment of adolescent happiness in a sinful love. We have noted that, as a propitiatory gesture, Charles's wicked father-enemy is not his father (as he well might have been) but his thoroughly aristocratic twin-uncle, who, being French, is more villainous than any British father-enemy might have been. Mr. Stryver, in his vampirish relationship with Carton, is another figure of the worthless "father" who sucks the blood of his talented "son." And since Dickens almost always maintains a balance between evil and virtuous figures in all categories, we have, on the benevolent side, Mr. Lorry, another unmarried "father," the only living figure in the gallery of scarecrows who inhabit Tellson's Bank. Mid-

way between the two classes is the hagridden Ernest Defarge, whose every attempt at benevolence is thwarted by his
vengeful wife and her abettors, the allegorically named
Vengeance and the members of the society of Jacques. This
last-named group produces one brilliantly sketched psy-
chopath, the sadistic, finger-chewing Jacques Three.

The one remaining father figure is the most interesting,
complex, and well-developed character in the whole novel,
Dr. Manette. Since he could not have been much more than
twenty-five years old when he was torn from his newly-
wedded English wife to be imprisoned in the Bastille for
nearly eighteen years, he must have been less than forty-five
when we first met him in Defarge's garret. And Dickens, let
it be remembered, was forty-five when he wrote of him.
Here is his portrait:

> A broad ray of light fell into the garret, and showed the work-
> man, with an unfinished shoe upon his lap, pausing in his
> labour. His few common tools and various scraps of leather
> were at his feet and on his bench. He had a white beard,
> raggedly cut, but not very long, a hollow face, and exceed-
> ingly bright eyes. The hollowness and thinness of his face
> would have caused them to look large, under his yet dark eye-
> brows and his confused white hair, though they had been re-
> ally otherwise; but they were naturally large, and looked un-
> naturally so. His yellow rags of shirt lay open at the throat,
> and showed his body to be withered and worn. (I, 6)

Of course the appearance of great age in a middle-age man
is rationally explained by the suffering entailed by his long,
unjust imprisonment. Yet, nearly eighteen years later (the
repetition of the number is meaningful), when he has become the unwitting agent of his son-in-law's destruction and
has been unable to use his special influence to procure
Charles' release, he is pictured as a decayed mass of senility.

> "Who goes here? Whom have we within? Papers!"
> The papers are handed out and read.
> "Alexandra Manette. Physician. French. Which is he?"
> This is he; this helpless, inarticulately murmuring, wan-
> dering old man pointed out.
> "Apparently the Citizen-Doctor is not in his right mind?
> The Revolution-fever will have been too much for him?"
> Greatly too much for him. (III, 13)

Carton envisions his complete recovery, but we have some
difficulty in believing it.

In the interim, however, he is pictured as a stalwart,
middle-aged medical practitioner. His sufferings have caused

a period of amnesia, with occasional flashes of painful recollection, as in the scene in which he hears of the discovery of a stone marked D I G in a cell in the Tower of London. We never know, by the way, whether his recollection at this moment is complete and whether he has, even furtively, any recall of the existence of the document of denunciation found by M. Defarge. The aspects of conscious and repressed memory are here handled with great skill by Dickens. Generally, his amnesia is reciprocal; he cannot recall his normal life during the period of relapse, or vice versa, especially when his relapses are triggered by events and disclosures which bring up memories of his old wrongs. His reversion to shoemaking for a short time after Charles proposes marriage to Lucie and again for a longer time following Lucie's marriage and Charles's final revelation of his long-suspected identity foreshadow the great disclosure which is to make him the unwitting aggressor against the happiness of his loving and beloved daughter. . . .

A DISTURBING FANTASY?

A Tale of Two Cities does, it seems to me, give every indication, even apart from its past history, that it "can please many and please long." Its use of the dynamic scapegoat pattern with the employment of the pattern of multiple projection, which it has been my aim to point out in this essay, does indeed embody a fantasy, a fantasy which was disturbing to Dickens and is still undoubtedly disturbing to many readers, and has used that device of multiple projection as the defensive maneuver that enables readers to master that disturbance. In that sense, there seems to be little doubt about the continuance of the perennial popularity of this often maligned but still frequently read novel of Dickens' later period.

But all of that is really by the way. Criticism of the kind which I have attempted is designed to furnish information rather than critical judgment, even of a prognostic nature; it is the kind of criticism which was described by Arthur Symons in his introduction to the *Biographia Literaria* of Coleridge:

> The aim of criticism is to distinguish what is essential in the work of a writer. It is the delight of the critic to praise; but praise is scarcely part of his duty. . . . What we ask of him is that he should find out for us more than we can find out for ourselves.

Charles Darnay: A Most Unromantic Romantic Hero

Edwin M. Eigner

In the following essay, Edwin M. Eigner argues that
Charles Darnay is more a comic stock character of
the Harlequin type than a revolutionary hero.
Eigner's reference is to the characters of the commedia dell'arte, a style of improvised theatrical satire
that became extremely popular in Europe in the sixteenth century. The commedia, which featured several masked stock characters, including the young
maiden Columbine, the aging and naive merchant
Pantaloon, and the shrewd and impudent servant
Harlequin, had a strong influence on modern theater, particularly, as Eigner points out, on English
Victorian pantomimes of the 1800s. In the latter pre-
sentations, the character of Harlequin had developed
into Columbine's lover; and it is after this version of
Harlequin, suggests Eigner, that Dickens patterned
Darnay. As Harlequin always manages to do, Darnay
escapes serious trouble, but his good luck is more
than offset by his blandness, powerlessness, and
guilt. Eigner is a scholar and member of the editorial
board of the journal *Dickens Studies Annual.*

As early as . . . *Nicholas Nickleby* in 1838, Dickens structured
each of his novels on a form of popular entertainment called
the Christmas or Easter Pantomime. Dickens' Pantomime is
not to be confused either with the sort of thing [modern
mime artist] Marcel Marceau does or with the cheap enter-
tainments called pantomimes or pantos which are staged
these days in England every Christmas season, although
both are descendants. The Regency and Early Victorian Pantomime which influenced Dickens was a highly stylized af-

Excerpted from "Charles Darnay and Revolutionary Identity" by Edwin M. Eigner,
Dickens Studies Annual, vol. 12 (1983), pp. 147-57. Reprinted by permission of AMS
Press, New York, N.Y.

fair, always in two parts. In the first and relatively realistic scene, a pair of young lovers would have their romantic plans frustrated by three characters: the girl's avaricious or weak father, a wicked or foppish lover whom the father favors, and a blundering comic servant. When the wicked lover seems about to triumph, a benevolent spirit out of Mother Goose or the Arabian Nights or some other fantasy appears and changes each of the characters into one of the figures from the English development of the *commedia dell arte* Harlequinade. The girl becomes Columbine, the boy she loves becomes Harlequin, the father is changed to Pantaloon, the wicked lover is transformed to a figure called Dandy Lover, and the servant becomes Clown, who is the ancestor of Charles Chaplin and the circus and rodeo clowns of today. These transformations give the young lovers another chance, with the odds in their favor this time, for Harlequin is nimbler than his enemies and he is aided by a magic bat or slap-stick. He is also the beneficiary of the actions of Clown, who either intentionally or inadvertently betrays his masters, Pantaloon and Dandy Lover, and saves the young people. This is done at his own expense, not only because he receives blows from his master but, frequently, because he is himself in love with Columbine.

My argument is that most Dickens heroines find themselves surrounded by four would-be lovers, who correspond to the four male figures in the Harlequinade. She always has a father or a father figure who gets her into trouble, sometimes by selfishly exploiting her, as in *Nicholas Nickleby*, but more often unintentionally, as with Dr. Manette in *A Tale of Two Cities*, or at least without any consciously wicked intention. I make this last qualification because there is frequently the suggestion, as with Manette again, that the father's feeling for his daughter is not purely parental and that he views her favored lover, Charles Darnay in this novel, with more than a touch of sexual jealousy. Consciously, Manette means nothing but good for Charles, and he is sincerely active in his attempts to free him, but the efforts fail, after all, and it is, of course, Manette's testimony, written in the Bastille, which condemns Charles.

The heroine has also a wicked lover, whose principal crime is usually an aspiration to rise in the social world by unfair or crass means until he achieves the bliss of winning her. Lawyer Stryver of *A Tale of Two Cities* is a weak embodiment of this figure from the Dickens Pantomime. . . .

Stryver is like these wicked lovers because he perceives the heroine as the reward, not as the means of his elevation—he is rather proud, in fact, of his decision to please himself and marry a poor girl. He is also like the others in that his shouldering self-assertiveness and vulgar determination to rise in life represent or reflect a chief evil which the novel exposes. From one point of view, at least, social mobility at any price is what the French Revolution is all about.

CHARLES DARNAY COMPARED TO RICHARD CARSTONE

Eigner points out that Richard Carstone, a good-hearted but weak and foolish young man in Dickens's novel Bleak House, *is in many ways equivalent to Darnay in* Tale. *Following is the introductory description of Carstone from* Bleak House, *and for comparison, Darnay's first description from* Tale.

The young gentleman was her distant cousin, she told me, and his name Richard Carstone. He was a handsome youth, with an ingenuous face, and a most engaging laugh; and after she had called him up to where we sat, he stood by us, in the light of the fire too, talking gaily, like a light-hearted boy. He was very young; not more than nineteen then, if quite so much, but nearly two years older than she was.

•   •   •   •   •

The object of all this staring and blaring, was a young man of about five-and-twenty, well-grown and well-looking, with a sunburnt cheek and a dark eye. His condition was that of a young gentleman. He was plainly dressed in black, or very dark grey, and his hair, which was long and dark, was gathered in a ribbon at the back of his neck; more to be out of his way than for ornament. . . . He was otherwise quite self-possessed, bowed to the Judge, and stood quiet.

The sort of interest with which this man was stared and breathed at, was not a sort that elevated humanity. Had he stood in peril of a less horrible sentence . . . by just so much would he have lost in his fascination.

Stryver is typical of this figure once again in that he employs, in a virtual slave capacity, the most dissipated and improvident of all the characters of the novel, a personage whom no one regards seriously and from whom no one ever expects anything, but who, like the Clown in the Harlequinade, always performs the essential action which saves the heroine. It was this character . . . finding most serious

expression in Sydney Carton of *A Tale of Two Cities*, which
... possessed the Saturnalian or sexual energy which be-
longed in the Pantomime Harlequinade to Clown rather
than Harlequin, [and therefore] was able to act where the romantic lover, from whom one would naturally expect action,
was powerless. ... In *A Tale of Two Cities* it is the unre-
garded Sydney Carton who can act decisively in the crisis,
while his much more successful and substantial rival,
Charles Darnay, has been powerless, powerless not only to
defend himself from the revengeful fury of the revolution,
but also impotent to protect his family, to avoid being caught
in the machinations of his wicked uncle, to benefit the starving peasants on his French estate, and, perhaps most significantly, to carry out the first charge of his life, laid upon him
by his mother when he was a boy, to find and care for the
sister of the raped girl, Madame Defarge, who has little trouble finding and taking care of him.

WHY DARNAY IS SO DISLIKED

It is this figure, the romantic lover, on whom I wish to concentrate . . for just as Sydney Carton was the least funny
and the most significant of Dickens' Clowns, so Charles Darnay is the most heavy-footed and, certainly to this point of
the author's career, the most problematic of his Harlequins.

Readers and critics, until recently, at any rate, have found
Dickens' romantic heroes among the least interesting of his
characters, and Darnay is certainly no exception in this regard. He has differed from the other heroes who end up with
the girls, however, in that, from the beginning, and in spite
of the facts that his manners are impeccable and usually calculated not to give offense, he has inspired animosity both
from those within the novel and those outside it. ... It is un-
derstandable, I suppose, that Madame Defarge and the revolutionaries should see Charles, whether mistakenly or not,
as their enemy, the symbol of their oppression. Even the Old
Bailey crowd in England can perhaps be excused for their
disappointment at not getting to see him half-hanged, then
taken down and sliced before his own face, then have his insides burnt while he looks on, then have his head chopped
off, and then have his body cut into quarters. Maybe there is
not anything personal in this. One could not hope, moreover,
that Charles would be especially popular with his English
romantic rivals. It is to be expected, therefore, that Stryver

should "believe there is contamination in such a scoundrel" and that Carton should simply "hate the fellow." Nor should we be surprised at the negative feelings of those millions of readers who have identified with Carton and felt his rejection by Lucie as if it were their own. Even Charles is quick to excuse his father-in-law for condemning him and his descendants "to the last of their race." It's what he's come to expect. Nevertheless, some of the dislike for Darnay goes beyond the explanations provided. . . .

I think an answer to [the] question . . . of why Charles is so disliked within the novel may lie in the way this hero regards himself. Darnay's self-contempt is not so . . . obvious as Carton's, but I suspect it is deeper and more difficult to transcend, at least by his own efforts. Think, for instance, of the meek way he accepts Carton's insolence after the English trial and the modest way he presses his claim to Lucie when he asks her father not to oppose his courtship.

> I have felt [he says], and do feel even now, that to bring my love—even mine—between you [and Lucie], is to touch your history with something not quite so good as itself.

At the level of the book's religious allegory, he is, of course, Everyman, suffering from original sin. . . . He is guilty also of a kind of parricide, having imagined or willed the death of his father's twin brother, the evil Marquis, just hours or perhaps minutes before the latter's murder. But one does not need a Christian or a Freudian interpretation to understand the guilt feelings of a man who was told by his mother when he was two years old that unless he can find and reconcile the needle-in-a-haystack sister of the peasant girl his father had wronged, "atonement would one day be required of him." Moreover, guilt is a speciality of the romantic hero in Dickens' later novels.

LUCK AND GUILT

In the essays he wrote about the Pantomime at various points in his career, Dickens had interesting things to say about most of the figures, but Harlequin was described only as an ordinary man "to be found in no particular walk or degree, on whom a certain station, or particular conjunction of circumstances, confers the magic wand." In other words, he is lucky enough to be loved by Columbine, and this luck seems to be the one most significant aspect of the character Dickens derived from Harlequin. Two years after the publication of the essay in question, when he was driving towards the conclusion of *Nicholas Nickleby* and setting up what I believe to be the first pantomime within his fiction, Dickens had pantaloon-wearing Ralph Nickleby say of his Harlequin nephew, "There is some spell about that boy.... Circumstances conspire to help him. Talk of fortune's favours! What is even money to such Devil's luck as this?" Thus began, if it did not begin even earlier in *Oliver Twist*, a line of Dickens heroes who narrowly escape death in war or by plague or shipwreck or attempted murder or who are selected arbitrarily to become gentlemen.... In *The Frozen Deep*, the Wilkie Collins–Charles Dickens play which inspired the writing of *A Tale of Two Cities*, Richard Wardour, the model for Sydney Carton, says contemptuously to the man whom he has not yet recognized as his rival but for whom he will ultimately sacrifice his own life, "You have got what the women call a lucky face." And Carton himself regards Charles Darnay similarly when he reflects, "I thought he was rather a handsome fellow, and I thought I should have been much the same sort of fellow if I had had any luck."

Charles is, of course, not only lucky in his face and in love and in his Harlequin knack of always getting out or being gotten out of the deadly scrapes he finds himself in, he is also extremely lucky in his birth as compared to his starving French countrymen. This last mentioned aspect of his luck, moreover, is what relates him most closely to other Dickens heroes and to the guilty feeling heroes in a number of important nineteenth- and twentieth-century novels.... From very early in his career, from at least as early as *Martin Chuzzlewit*, Dickens tended to combine the luck of his Harlequin figures, the romantic lovers, with feelings of guilt. ... Pip, the romantic hero of [*Great Expectations*,] which follows *A Tale of Two Cities*, is similarly successful in getting rid of the shame he has been made to feel in his youth by parlaying it into real guilt, guilt at having snobbishly rejected the people who are dearest to him, and especially at not having rejected the destructive metaphor current in the novel which divides humanity into genteel predators— hounds or spiders—and impoverished victims—varmints or insects—instead of acknowledging everyone, as Joe Gargery does, as a fellow creature. Pip is, of course, both the luckiest and the guiltiest of the romantic heroes, lucky enough to get a fortune merely by wishing for it, and so guilty that Dickens could not make up his mind in the first draft of the novel to let him marry the heroine.

DARNAY'S POWERLESSNESS

On the other hand, Charles Darnay does most emphatically get the girl, although, as we have seen, she is virtually the only character in *A Tale of Two Cities*, including himself, who can stand him. Charles's marriage, in fact, occurs in the sixteenth of the thirty-one serial parts of the novel, that is to say, the very center, always the place of highest significance in a Dickens story. "Charles Darnay's way," we are told by the author, is the one way "the world of man has invariably gone . . . the way of the love of a woman." He is so lucky that even the immense power of his sense of guilt and unworthiness has no ultimate force against him.

Nevertheless, we ought not to underestimate the depth of that sense of guilt, and we should, I think, give due attention to the question of how far it is justified in relation to the principal action and historical event of *A Tale of Two Cities*: the French Revolution; that is to say, how much of Charles Darnay's guilt is not only an expression of the condition of man after the Fall and of undeniable psychological trauma, but is caused and perhaps justified by Charles's failures as social man.

To begin with, he has not fulfilled the first charge of his life, to sell his mother's jewels and give the money to the sister of the raped peasant girl, Madame Defarge, as it turns out. In fact, we are not told that Charles so much as made an attempt at carrying out this obligation, although it is possible that this is what he was trying to do on those mysterious trips between England and France between 1775 and 1780. This is special pleading in Charles's behalf, for there is no evidence, but I can think of no other explanation for the secrecy of these journeys, a secrecy which, at his English trial for treason, Charles maintains at very serious expense to his case and danger to his life. He told Lucie he "was travelling under an assumed name" because he "was travelling on a business of a delicate and difficult nature, which might get people into trouble." He could not have been divesting himself of his estate, for he had not come into that yet, and it is difficult to imagine who, besides himself and anti-aristocratic agents helping in the search for the wronged girl, might be in any danger. Still it is curious that Dickens maintains the secrecy, and curious also that Darnay, usually so apt to feel guilty, does not torture himself about this failure to carry out his mother's first command.

On the other hand, Darnay is distraught at his powerlessness to, as he says, "execute the last request of my dear mother's lips, and obey the last look of my dear mother's eyes, which implored me to have mercy and to redress." The powerlessness comes, presumably, from Charles's situation of having been passed over in the inheritance—his wicked uncle rules instead of him—but when he does succeed to the estate, just hours after making this speech, he is still unable to perform effectively:

> He had acted imperfectly. He knew very well, that in his love for Lucie, his renunciation of his social place, though by no means new to his mind, had been hurried and incomplete. He knew that he ought to have systematically worked it out and supervised it, and that he had meant to do it, and that it had never been done . . . he had watched the times for a time of action . . . until the time had gone by.

But even this confession of failure by Charles misses the point. Presumably his mother's lips and eyes had not implored him to renounce his power, but rather to use it for the sake of the poor. . . .

In the second place, Charles's impulsive action is strongly reminiscent of the ineffective or unsustained windmill charges on social institutions made by previous romantic heroes in Dickens' novels. He dashes into the French Revolution as Arthur Clennam of *Little Dorrit* took on the Circumlocution Office or as Richard Carstone of *Bleak House* smashed his head against the Court of Chancery. The action is naively vain, as Dickens suggests when he tells us of Darnay that the "glorious vision of doing good, which is so often the sanguine mirage of so many good minds, arose before him, and he even saw himself in the illusion with some influence to guide this raging Revolution." And there is also the possibility of an unworthy subconscious motivation for his action. Since it developed from a sense of shame and guilt, Charles's purpose, like that of Clennam, may be to punish himself. Having failed to redress the wrong as his mother had charged him to do, he may be embracing the opportunity for the violent atonement she had predicted as the alternative. In any event, these are the ways Charles's brief career as a social activist seems destined to turn out—vain and self-destructive.

THREE WEDDINGS

But before we go too far in joining the chorus which condemns Charles Darnay, it is well to remember that Dickens could never bring himself to believe in the Carlylean hero and that by this time in his career he was highly skeptical of the effectuality of social action of any sort. Dickens may not be criticizing Charles Darnay's qualities as a Revolutionary hero; he is more likely undermining the very concept of romantic heroism by doubting both its motives and its possibilities for success. Charles is at least as powerless in Revolutionary France as he was in bourgeois England, but in the long run he is no less effectual than the other would-be Revolutionary heroes whose fate Carton predicts in the final chapter. . . .

Charles Darnay is rendered physically powerless by the Revolution he had come to France to direct, and he is transformed into a helpless and sleeping infant by the growing strength of Sydney Carton. Nevertheless, he keeps a firm hold on his role as Harlequin. I suggested earlier that the action of the sixteenth number, the wedding of Charles and Lucie, pointed to marriage as the novel's central meaning. Other places one looks for meaning in a Dickens novel are the earliest and latest points of the story. . . . In Dickens' earliest manuscript, the younger Evremonde twin did not rape the peasant girl; he seduced her by pretending to marry her. So the story was intended also to begin with a marriage, albeit a false one. I think *A Tale of Two Cities* ends with a marriage, as well, the marriage of Carton and the little seamstress, whose innocence and occupation identify her as a substitute for Lucie of the golden thread. The three weddings indicate a progress: we begin with a false and secret marriage; move then to the real but strangely private nuptials of Charles and Lucie; and conclude with a wedding which is both symbolic and highly public. This wedding on the scaffold validates Carton and his great sacrifice. He is dying for Darnay and for Darnay's marriage to Lucie. It is perhaps of equal significance that in an unrendered scene of the novel which presumably took place at La Force Prison, Charles Darnay courted Sydney Carton's bride for him. When the girl approaches Sydney and asks if she can hold his hand in the cart, she still mistakes him for his double, whom both he and the reader have neglected to thank, and whose identity, revolutionary and otherwise, is as Harlequin lover.

Dr. Manette's Escape from Prison to Freedom

Jack Lindsay

Most scholars identify Sydney Carton as the pivotal character in *A Tale of Two Cities*. By contrast, in this essay by well-known historian, archaeologist, biographer, and literary critic Jack Lindsay, the key character is Dr. Manette. The fate of this "lost man," says Lindsay, symbolizes the struggle of the masses in the French Revolution and therefore lies at the novel's core. In Lindsay's view, Manette also symbolizes the stressful and emotional ordeal Dickens himself was undergoing at the time he conceived the novel. Supposedly, Dickens projected his own character into the story, not only in the guise of Carton and Darnay, as many argue, but also in the form of Dr. Manette, a man, like Dickens, attempting to break out of a confined and miserable existence.

Charles Dickens was in a driven demoniac state of mind when the idea for *A Tale of Two Cities* came to him. The bracelet he sent to [the young actress] Ellen Lawless Ternan had fallen into the hands of his wife Kate; and he was determined to end his marriage and to seduce Ellen. But he was in the midst of the rehearsals which had finally brought himself and Ellen together; and he could not pause to think. Amid Kate's tears, [his friend John] Forster's disapproval and a generally unnerving situation, he carried on in his furious possessed fashion, determined to have his own way and yet to keep his hold on the public; and in the midst of this spiritually and physically racked condition, as he was holding back his agony of mind by acting and producing [Wilkie Collins's play] *The Frozen Deep*, the central idea of the novel burst upon him.

From Jack Lindsay, "A Tale of Two Cities," in *Life and Letters*, vol. 62 (July-September, 1949), pp. 191-204. Copyright ©1949 by Jack Lindsay. Reprinted by permission of David Higham Associates, London, on behalf of the author's estate.

So much we know from his own statement. It is clear then that we should be able to find the imprint of his ordeal, his tormented choice, in the novel. One would expect writers on his work to concentrate on this problem; but so abysmally low is the standard of Dickens criticism that no one has even seriously raised the question at all.

THE LOST AND FORGOTTEN MAN

Where then is the imprint of the situation to be traced? By solving this point we can begin to understand what the novel itself is about, and the part it plays in Dickens's development. One general aspect of the selection of theme is at once obvious. The deep nature of the breach he is making with all customary acceptances is driving him to make a comprehensive effort to grasp history in a new way. So far (except for *Barnaby Rudge*) he has been content to use certain symbols to define his sense of basic historical conflict and movement. Yet all the while the influence of [his friend, the noted historian Thomas] Carlyle, both in his *French Revolution* and his prophetic works like *Past and Present*, has been stirring him with the need for a direct statement of the historical issue as well as a symbolic one; and now, as he is coming close to a full confrontation of his opposition to all ruling Victorian values, he feels the need to set his story of conflicting wills in a manifestly revolutionary situation: that on which he had so long pondered as holding the clue to the crisis of his own world.

He had read and re-read Carlyle's history, till its theme and material were richly present in his mind; and now he wrote to the master asking for a loan of the cited authorities. The story goes that Carlyle jokingly sent him all his reference books, "about two cartloads." And in the novel's preface Dickens wrote:

> It has been one of my hopes to add something to the popular and picturesque means of understanding that terrible time, though no one can hope to add anything to the philosophy of Mr. Carlyle's wonderful book.

But though this need to make a general reconsideration of the nature of historical movement and change was certainly central in the impulse that Dickens felt, he had to fuse the overt theme with a more immediately personal nexus of emotion and imagery before it could take full grip of him. In the midst of his domestic misery and frenzied play-acting he did not feel simply an intellectual need to revalue history. The desire to break through obstructions and to mate with Ellen could turn into the desire to write about the French Revolution only if some image or symbol made him feel a basic coincidence between his own experience and the Revolution. What then was this image?

It was that of the Imprisoned Man in the Bastille. The Lost Man who had been jailed so long that he has become an automaton of oppressed misery; who has forgotten even the source of his wrong, the cause of his dehumanizing misery; who needs to break out of the deadly darkness of stone in order to become human again, to learn the truth and regain love.

Here then is the core of the novel. The originally-intended title was *Recalled to Life*. Though Dickens dropped this for the whole novel, he kept it for the first part, and it expressed the originating emotion of the story. *A Tale of Two Cities* is built up from the episode of Dr. Manette's unjust imprisonment; and its whole working-out is concerned with the effects of that unjust deprivation of light and joy: effects which entangle everyone round the Doctor and recoil back on his own head in unpredictable ways. The Doctor's fate is thus for Dickens both a symbol of the Revolution, its deeds, causes, and consequences, and of himself, immured in a maddening cell of lies and cruelties, and seeking to break through into the truth, into a full and happy relationship with his fellows. It was the demented sense of environing pressures, of an unjust inescapable mechanism, which caught Dickens up in the midst of his wild mummery and gave him a sense of release when he determined to write the novel.

THE OLD MUST DIE FOR THE NEW

It has been pointed out . . . that there is a close underlying similarity between the plot of *A Tale* and that of *Little Dorrit* (the preceding novel in which Dickens had at last fully marshaled his condemnation of Victorian society). Both Dorrit and Manette are imprisoned for a score of years; both are released by forces outside their control and then continue tormented by their jail-experience. Dorrit is haunted by fear of social exposure, which comes finally in the collapse of Merdle (the exposure of the theft basic in the economic system). Dorrit thus from one angle embodies Dickens's deep fears of the past, fears of being exposed, fears of being driven back

on the terrible moment of loss which therefore threatens to
return in exacerbated form. He also embodies the bad conscience of a whole society which dares not contemplate truly
its origins. But in Manette the symbolism goes much deeper.
The experience of oppressive misery has not merely twisted
him, as it twisted Dorrit; it has broken down the whole system of memory in his psyche. The problem then is: What can
restore consciousness? what can connect the upper and the

THE CHILD OF THE MARSHALSEA

Like Dr. Manette, Dorrit, the central character in Dickens's
Little Dorrit, *endures years of unjust imprisonment, an experience that shapes the remainder of her life. In the following
excerpt, Dorrit, whom Dickens refers to as the Child of the
Marshalsea (for Marshalsea Prison, where her father has
been jailed for debt), becomes grimly habituated to prison life.*

With a pitiful and plaintive look for everything indeed, but
with something in it for only him that was like protection,
this Child of the Marshalsea and child of the Father of the
Marshalsea, sat by her friend the turnkey in the lodge, kept
the family room, or wandered about the prison-yard, for the
first eight years of her life. With a pitiful and plaintive look
for her wayward sister; for her idle brother; for the high
blank walls; for the faded crowd they shut in; for the games
of the prison children as they whooped and ran, and played
at hide-and-seek, and made the iron bars of the inner gate-
way 'Home.'...

This was the life, and this the history, of the Child of the
Marshalsea, at twenty-two. With a still surviving attachment
to the one miserable yard and block of houses as her birth-
place and home, she passed to and fro in it shrinkingly now,
with a womanly consciousness that she was pointed out to
every one. Since she had begun to work beyond the walls,
she had found it necessary to conceal where she lived, and
to come and go as secretly as she could, between the free
city and the iron gates, outside of which she had never slept
in her life. Her original timidity had grown with this concealment, and her light step and her little figure shunned
the thronged streets while they passed along them....

This was the life, and this the history, of Little Dorrit ...
turning at the end of London Bridge, recrossing it, going
back again, passing on to Saint George's Church, turning
back suddenly once more, and flitting in at the open outer
gate and little court-yard of the Marshalsea.

hidden levels of the mind again? Manette is kept going by a blind exercise of the craft learned in the cell of oppression, and only the intrusion of events from the Revolution can bring him back to an active consciousness and release him from his obsession. But the drama of objectifying in action the pattern of memory, the repetition-compulsion which must be broken, inevitably brings its shocks, its apparent evocation of forces as destructive as those working from the traumatic level. The test lies in the way that evocation is faced, the way it works out. So Manette finds that the bitterness engendered by his sufferings as an innocent wronged man has tangled him up in a net (inside a larger reference of social action and reaction, guilt and innocence) from which escape is possible only after a great sacrifice has been made. The old must die for the new to be born; man cannot attain regeneration without accepting its sacrificial aspect. In the story this appears in the struggle between Darnay and Carton for Manette's daughter, and the solution that mates Darnay and the girl, yet sends Carton to a regeneration in death.

In this dire tangle of moral consequences we see Dickens confronting his own confused situation and trying to equate his own moment of painful compelled choice with the revolutionary moment in which a definite break is made with the old, amid violent birthpangs, and makes possible the rebirth of life, the renewal of love and innocence.

The lacerated and divided state of Dickens's emotions at this moment of choice is revealed by the device of having two heroes who are practically twins in appearance and who love the same girl. Both Carton and Darnay are generous fellows, but one is morally well-organized, the other is fecklessly a misfit. The latter, however, by his devoted death reaches the same level of heroic generosity as his rival; indeed goes higher. His gesture of renunciation completes the ravages of the Revolution with its ruthless justice, and transforms them into acts of purification and redemption, without which the life of renewed love would not be possible.

Thus, in the story, Dickens gets the satisfaction of nobly giving up the girl and yet mating with her. He splits himself in the moment of choice, dies, and yet lives to marry the beloved, from whom the curse born out of a tainted and divided society is at last removed. And at the same time he is Manette, the man breaking out of a long prison-misery, who seeks only truth and justice, and whose submerged memory-drama projects itself as both the Carton-Darnay conflict and the socially-impinging dilemma that disrupts and yet solves that conflict.

WORKING OUT THE CLASH OF FORCES

There are thus a number of ambivalences in the story; and Dickens shows himself divided in his attitude to the Revolution itself. His petty-bourgeois fear of mass-movements is still alive; but the fascination of such movements, which stirred so strongly in *Barnaby*, is even keener than the fear. On the one hand he clings to the moral thesis to defend the Revolution: the Old Regime was vilely cruel and bestialized people, it could not but provoke excesses in return as the bonds slipped. But this thesis, to which Carlyle had sought to give a grandiose religious tang, now merges for Dickens with a deeper acceptance. . . .

Throughout the book there runs this ambivalent attitude to the Revolution, shuddering, yet inclining to a deep and thorough acceptance. Not a blank-cheque acceptance, but one based on the subtle dialectics of conflict revealed by the story of Manette. For that story, symbolizing the whole crisis and defining its tensions in the depths of the spirit, makes a serious effort to work out the process of change, the rhythms of give-and-take, the involved struggles with their many inversions and opposed refractions, the ultimate resolution in death and love, in the renewal of life.

The working-out of the clash of forces is in fact more thoroughly done than in any previous work of Dickens. The weakness lies in the comparative thinness of characterization. The strain of grasping and holding intact the complex skein of the story is too much for Dickens at this difficult moment of growth. But his instinct is, as always, right. He needed this strenuous effort to get outside himself: no other way could he master the difficult moment and rebuild his foundations. After it he could return to the attack on the contemporary world with a new sureness, with new thews of drama, with new breadths of comprehension. The great works, *Great Expectations* and *Our Mutual Friend*, were made possible. (I am not here dealing with those works; but it is interesting to note that the imprisonment-theme finds its completion in the contrasted and entangled themes of Miss Havisham and the old convict [in *Great Expectations*], the self-imposed prison of the traumatic moment and the socially-imposed prison of the criminal impulse, both merging to express the compulsions of an acquisitive society.)

A Tale is not a successful work like the two novels that followed it, but they would never have been written without it. An inner strain appears in the rigidity of tension between the thematic structure and the release of character-fantasy. Such persons as Manette, however, show a new persistence of psychological analysis, and the Defarges show what untapped sources of dramatic force Dickens could yet draw on. The final falsification of the book's meaning came about through the melodrama based on its material, in which the emphasis put on Carton sentimentalized away all the profundities.

Lucie is meant to represent Ellen Ternan; but at this stage Dickens knows very little about the real Ellen, and Lucie is therefore a stock-heroine. Charles Darnay, the winning lover, has the revealing initials *Charles D*. Dickens with his love of name-meanings can seldom resist leaving at least one or two such daydream-admissions among the names of a novel. Ellen was acting as Lucy in *The Frozen Deep* at the time when the novel's idea came. . . .

An examination then of the inner movement of symbolism in *A Tale* . . . makes sufficiently clear the potence of the image that burst on Dickens in the midst of his personal crisis. The examination reveals important subtleties that have been ignored or explained away in the general movement of falsification which has held appalling sway . . . in the realm of Dickens "criticism." *A Tale* is not a great work, though like almost anything written by Dickens it has great elements; but when it is seriously approached, it turns out to be a work of high interest yielding some essential clues to the workings of Dickens's mind and of creative symbolism in general.

The Members of Dickens's Crowd Act as a Single Character

David Craig

The following essay is written by David Craig, a senior lecturer in English literature at Lancaster University. In it, Craig examines Dickens's use of angry mobs in *A Tale of Two Cities*. In comparison with the crowd in Dickens's other historical novel, *Barnaby Rudge*, which Dickens describes as "a mad monster," Craig points out that in *Tale*, a more mature work than *Rudge*, Dickens's crowd has become more of a "class" than a "motley mob." All of these descriptions suggest that the crowd, like other distinct characters in these works, serves a purpose, acts out a part, and effects an outcome. In Craig's opinion, Dickens's treatment of the crowd as a faceless mass devoid of individuality was typical of socially conscious novelists of the Victorian era.

Dickens's two main visions of the epoch just before his birth, *Barnaby Rudge* (1841) and *A Tale of Two Cities* (1859), both have at their centre an image of the mass of the people looting, burning, injuring, killing, and destroying even themselves. The Gordon Riot of 1780, in London, and the French Revolution of 1789–91, in Paris, are presented as unrelieved scenes of demonic and bestial behaviour. . . .

Barnaby Rudge is much the simpler of the two novels in its conception of how 'mobs' accumulate and behave, much the more swingeing in its low view of militant crowds. The anti-Catholic rioters are stirred up by 'the worst passions of the worst men'. For those few days in June 1780, Londoners were in a state of 'mania', which was all the more intense because the grounds for it were so flimsy; and once the rioting had started, a 'moral plague ran through the city' which

Excerpted from "The Crowd in Dickens" by David Craig, in *The Changing World of Charles Dickens*, edited by Robert Giddings (London: Vision Press, 1983), pp. 75-88. Reprinted by permission of Alkin Books, Ltd., London.

made even 'sober workmen' drop their toolbags on their way home and join the crowds who were smashing house-fronts and burning roofs and furniture. . . . The crowd 'was composed for the most part of the very scum and refuse of London', of 'idle and profligate persons' whose behaviour was as 'terrible' and 'fickle' as the ocean. . . . 'The mob raged and roared, like a mad monster, as it was.'. . .

Such are the passages which prompt us most tellingly to take a judging view of the riotous townsfolk. The sheer evocation of their behaviour is for the most part graphically detailed and convincing. It engages Dickens's powers as the most talented journalist of his time. . . .

From such writing we can see distinctly how the crowd behaved. Why they did so is another matter—they do not experience, they merely behave, and their motives are only thinly accounted for. . . .

A VAST MASS OF SCARECROWS

A Tale of Two Cities offers a deeper account than *Barnaby Rudge* of how a rising gathers way. It is also more chastened and less righteous in its conception of destructive tendencies in social behaviour. A mature writer is at work now, and he has taken on a much more formidable subject—not a riot but a revolution. Again Dickens offers plenty of graphic descriptions of wrecking and killing, drawing heavily on Carlyle's *The French Revolution* (1837), which he had always greatly admired. But the rioters here are not a motley mass, they are a class, with motives shown to be rooted in their poverty and the cruelty of the landowners, epitomized in the running-down and killing of a slum child by the carriage of Monsieur le Marquis (II, 7). As such they are again evoked in imagery of the elemental, the bestial, the pathological. Again the crowd (the working men and women from the artisan district of Faubourg St.-Antoine, who storm the Bastille) are a 'sea of black and threatening waters', 'a vast dusky mass of scarecrows heaving to and fro', every person 'on high-fever strain and at high-fever heat', the women 'thirsting shrilly' for blood. . . .

The marked difference from *Barnaby Rudge* is the stress on poverty and injustice as causes of the degenerated behaviour. This link is explicit in a short key passage from the Bastille chapter:

The remorseless sea of turbulently swaying shapes, voices of vengeance, and faces hardened in the furnace of suffering until the touch of pity could make no mark on them.

We have already been prepared for this by the child's death and it now issues in the extraordinary sequence in the chapter called 'Fire Rises' which gives the form of myth to the links between the ill-used townsfolk and the starving peasantry, between France under the *ancien régime* (the novel opens, and the child is killed, in 1775) and the events of 1789 and after. The bereaved father turns into a 'shaggy-haired man of almost barbarian aspect' who wanders the countryside like an avenging spirit. By an unobtrusive device—shifting the verbs into the conditional mood—he is presented as not one but many:

> In these times, as the mender of roads worked, solitary, in the dust . . . he would see some rough figure approaching on foot, the like of which was once a rarity in those parts, but was now a frequent presence.

On this particular occasion road-mender and wanderer join hands and hint in monosyllables at an event set for the coming night. The road-mender exchanges his blue cap for a red one. And each calls the other 'Jacques'. Presently, from 'East, West, North, and South, through the woods, four heavy-treading, unkempt figures crushed the high grass and cracked the branches, striding on cautiously to come together in the court-yard' of the Marquis's château, and as it goes up in flames every villager sets a lighted candle in his window (II, 23). . . .

RIOTS SPANNING DECADES

What the stylization of 'Fire Rises' precludes is any fine focusing of sympathetic understanding on the revolutionaries. We are rarely close to, let alone inside, any suffering workman or peasant. The principal named revolutionaries are the Defarges and they are not in poverty. Neediness, starvation, ill-use, powerlessness remain generalized bad things which the liberal novelist can invoke from time to time. . . . Consider how different *A Tale of Two Cities* would have been if we had been put amongst the families crying and dying for want of bread and flour at a price they could afford—if we had seen at close quarters the mother, say, who killed two of her three children for fear of famine, the people who killed themselves for the same reason, or dropped dead in the Paris streets, or the women who gathered in the Bonnet de la Liberaté (Croix Rouge) and shouted 'Down with weapons! We want no more soldiers, because there is no more bread!' This was still happening in 1795, after some years of Revolutionary government, but well before that time Dickens has lost all sight of the values professed ever more desperately by the people who had made the Revolution. The centre of his stage is occupied (against a background of gibbering sadists) by the lonely noble martyrdom of Darnay/Carton, doing his better thing and going to his better place. . . .

A TEMPESTUOUS SEA OF PEOPLE

This brief excerpt from Barnaby Rudge, *in which young Barnaby finds himself swept along by a gathering mob, is a typical example of a Dickensian character finding him- or herself threatened by the ominous character of the faceless crowd.*

He went out into the street, so surrounded and hemmed in on every side by soldiers, that he could see nothing; but he knew there was a great crowd of people, by the murmur; and that they were not friendly to the soldiers, was soon rendered evident by their yells and hisses. . . .

As they came nearer and nearer to the prison, the hootings of the people grew more violent; stones were thrown; and every now and then, a rush was made against the soldiers, which they staggered under. One of them, close before him, smarting under a blow upon the temple, levelled his musket, but the officer struck it upwards with his sword, and ordered him on peril of his life to desist. This was the last thing he saw with any distinctness, for directly afterwards he was tossed about, and beaten to and fro, as though in a tempestuous sea. But go where he would, there were the same guards about him. Twice or thrice he was thrown down, and so were they; but even then, he could not elude their vigilance for a moment. They were up again, and had closed about him, before he, with his wrists so tightly bound, could scramble to his feet. Fenced in, thus, he felt himself hoisted to the top of a low flight of steps, and then for a moment he caught a glimpse of the fighting in the crowd, and of a few redcoats sprinkled together, here and there, struggling to rejoin their fellows. Next moment, everything was dark and gloomy, and he was standing in the prison lobby; the centre of a group of men.

Dickens is struggling to present, according to his lights, that most problematic social phenomenon, the militant

crowd. Such crowds were present in the lives of British people in his day to an extent we may now have to recover by efforts of historical imagination. The eighteenth and early
nineteenth century, says [historian] Edward Thompson [in
his book, *The Making of the English Working Class*], 'are
punctuated by riot, occasioned by bread prices, turnpikes
and tolls, excise, "rescue", strikes, new machinery, enclo-
sures, press-gangs and a score of other grievances'. The
commonest, he says, is 'the bread or food riot'. . . . In 1812,
the year of Dickens's birth, Luddism—the rising of "glovers,
stockingers, and other textile craftsmen against the powered
machines which were cheapening goods and undermining
their livelihoods—reached a peak. In 1812–13 forty men
were hanged for Luddite actions in the north of England
alone. In the summer of 1812 more than 12,000 troops were
stationed from York to Leicester. . . .

In France similar traditions prevailed, from the time of *la
guerre des farines* in the early 1770s, when loaves were
seized or bakers forced to sell them cheap, to the late '80s
and early '90s, when grain was seized from monasteries and
sugar, bread, meat, and wine were taken from warehouses
to be sold at low prices. . . .

NO JUSTIFICATION FOR VIOLENCE?

[Therefore] the terror which Dickens makes climactic in his
novel was in fact the last stage of an escalation whose pace
was forced relentlessly by successive governments and their
troops, Town Guards, and so on. The stages in this blur beneath Dickens's lurid imagery of a blood-curse working itself out. They are further obscured by the plot with its jumps
in time and from Paris to London and back again. Finally he
distorts the record by the propaganda device of mentioning
the atrocities done by one side only: e.g. during the siege of
the Bastille at least 150 citizens were killed against seven of
the garrison, but the only blood-letting Dickens brings fully
onto camera is the beheading of the governor. . . .

Here Dickens can get no further than the other outstand-
ing socially-conscious novelists of his time. . . . In their vision the crowd is a faceless mass—individuals are indistin-
guishable—the imagery which comes naturally to the
writers is of swarming or herding animals. It was early in
the nineteenth century that 'rookery' and 'warren' came
commonly to be used to mean congested, poor accommoda-

tion; an earlier meaning for 'warren' had been 'brothel'. This works in with the novelists' image of the workers erupting from the other end of town. When they do acquire individual faces, they are deformed, by violent passions, bad breeding, or disease. . . .

My point is that Dickens . . . [uses] this state of frightening collective fever to typify not only wild gangs but also workers' groups . . . who more likely than not would have been self-controlled.

Well before [Dickens] wrote, such faces and such motions were commonly attributed to townsfolk in the mass in the cartoons that [illustrators] Hogarth and Rowlandson, Gillray and Cruikshank made to be sold as prints. . . . That is to say, long before the Gordon Riot . . . the well-to-do already saw the common people as a barbarous horde, since this view of them was given, not so much from an actual history as from a longstanding syndrome of fears, worries, insecurities, on the part of the have's. It was replenished by each moment when the have-not's challenged them again. Today the syndrome lives on in . . . the Conservative Prime Minister who said after the Toxteth riot in June 1981 that unemployment was 'no justification' for the wrecking. The ethical term 'justification' evades the paramount social need, not to justify, but to explain the behaviour of people who do something which they would never do if they were in good heart and living well.

CHAPTER 3

The Treatment of Social and Historical Upheaval in *A Tale of Two Cities*

READINGS ON
A TALE OF TWO CITIES

Dickens's and Carlyle's Visions of an Inhumane Society

David D. Marcus

In the following essay, David D. Marcus, of the University of Illinois at Chicago Circle, examines Scottish historian Thomas Carlyle's influence on Dickens's writing of *A Tale of Two Cities*. Marcus contends that Carlyle often dealt with the theme of the individual seeking fulfillment in a society that has become devoid of humanity. Dickens developed this theme also, according to Marcus, by depicting humane characters caught in a relentless tide of historical and social processes that are blind to human needs and feelings. Though both condemned this inhumane system, Dickens and Carlyle recognized that social upheaval, exemplified by the French Revolution, is not the same as positive change; that is, such upheaval often results only in a recycling of the inhumane institutions of the past. In such cases, as Marcus puts it, the people cannot "break away from the enslaving spirit of their history."

A Tale of Two Cities is the most disparaged and least understood of Dickens's late novels. Overwhelmingly, the critics have judged the work a failure and dismissed it as intellectually superficial. According to this view, Dickens held only the most simpleminded view of history, and although the novel fictionalizes events whose memory haunted the Victorian era, it never places those events in the context of a coherent understanding of the processes of social change; the book is an amalgam of romantic melodrama based on Dickens's experience as an actor in Wilkie Collins's *Frozen Deep* and fragments taken from Carlyle's *French Revolution*, a work from which Dickens unsystematically borrowed de-

Excerpted from "The Carlylean Vision of *A Tale of Two Cities*" by David D. Marcus, *Studies in the Novel*, vol. 8, no. 1 (Spring 1976). Copyright by the University of North Texas, 1976. Reprinted by permission of the publisher.

tails but not any conceptual framework. . . .

But in fact, the two plots are closely related, and that relationship points toward a much more complex vision of history than criticism has so far allowed. My discussion of this relationship will also suggest that Dickens's conceptual debt to Carlyle is much greater than recent criticism has recognized. Dickens and Carlyle share a common quest that informs the historical vision of *A Tale of Two Cities*: both writers seek ways in which people can socialize their energies in an age whose institutions seem at odds with any humanly valuable purpose. . . .

The humane man finds himself caught in the mechanism of historical processes that move according to their own laws and that destroy any possibility of useful action. It is precisely this tie between the social and the psychic that unites the romantic and revolutionary plots of *A Tale of Two Cities*. . . .

The English as well as the French episodes deal with the problem of historical dehumanization. At the end of the novel, Darnay and Dr. Manette retreat into the tranquillity of a secluded domestic circle, and that retreat has to be seen in the light of their failure as public men to influence the course of events. Thus their retreat and the quasi-religious redemption through love and self-sacrifice are actually strategies for coping with the characters' need to find a sense of fruitful relatedness in the face of the impossibility of solving social problems. For Dickens, the family and religion serve much the same function as religion and the corporate spirit did for Carlyle: they are means of humanizing the void left in the individual life by mechanistic social institutions.

In describing the relationship between Carlyle and Dickens, I am emphasizing the social and secular sides of Carlyle's works and his role as the interpreter of the Romantic tradition to Victorian England. . . . Whether Carlyle is historically the only source of Dickens's efforts at dealing with the problem of the individual's relationship to his culture is not strictly demonstrable, although Dickens's own sense of himself as a disciple of Carlyle's certainly lends an air of plausibility to such speculation.' But Carlyle did crystallize these problems for his age, and both men saw the crisis of their culture in similar terms. Thus Carlyle provides at the very least a useful model for understanding Dickens, and for seeing Dickens as the heir to the Romantic era's tendency to internalize historical phenomena. Like Carlyle and the Romantic poets, Dickens is concerned with defining the possibilities for self-fulfillment in a society whose institutions seem inimical to all that is distinctively human.

PIECES IN A LARGER HISTORICAL PATTERN

From the beginning of *A Tale of Two Cities*, Dickens concentrates on the difficulty of understanding public events for those immersed in them. The famous opening paragraph presents the reader with a series of neat antitheses that in sum offer confusion rather than clarity:

> It was the best of times, it was the worst of times, it was the age of wisdom, it was the age of foolishness, it was the age of belief, it was the epoch of incredulity, it was the season of Light, it was the season of Darkness, it was the spring of hope, it was the winter of despair, we had everything before us, we had nothing before us, we were all going direct to Heaven, we were all going direct the other way—in short, the period was so far like the present period, that some of its noisiest authorities insisted on its being received, for good or for evil, in the superlative degree of comparison only.

At first, this passage seems to be a direct authorial commentary, but the attribution of these extreme opinions to some of the age's "noisiest authorities" invites us to question whether the noisiest and most extreme authorities of any age are to be trusted. The patterned rhetoric of the passage reveals confusion rather than understanding. The difficulties of reaching any clear knowledge of one's own era emerge through the novelist's explicit comparison of the past to the present and through the irony that both history and the novelist lend to the eighteenth-century's view of itself: "In both countries [England and France] it was clearer than crystal to the lords of the State preserves of loaves and fishes, that things in general were settled for ever." As Dickens points out immediately afterwards, the year is 1775, and with both the American and French Revolutions impending, things in general are anything but settled forever. As the novel's first paragraph makes clear, both the age's noisiest authorities and its powers that be are unaware of the significance of the historical forces that are shaping the future.

Only in retrospect do events assume a clear order. The novel's French episodes invite the reader to view every incident in the light of his historical knowledge and to recognize events as pieces in a larger pattern that is known a priori [beforehand]. All of the French action appears first as a foreshadowing and later as a realization of the Revolution, and Dickens eschews subtlety in favor of a directness that always keeps before the reader the relationship of each action to larger historical forces. Thus the opening French scene with its broken wine cask flooding the street suggests in its sacramental overtones the blood that will one day flow in the streets; but Dickens is not content to leave matters at the level of suggestion: "The time was to come, when that wine too would be spilled on the street-stones, and when the stain of it would be red upon many there.". . .

Similarly, the French characters have no individuality but exist only to play their roles in the revolutionary drama. They are defined exclusively in terms of their class. Our first glimpse of the Marquis is at a reception at which he is singled out only after a very Carlylean critique of a degenerate aristocracy whose only function has become self-aggrandizement: "Military officers destitute of military knowledge; naval officers with no idea of a ship; civil officers without a notion of affairs; brazen ecclesiastics, of the worst world worldly . . . all totally unfit for their several callings, all lying horribly in pretending to belong to them, but all nearly or remotely of the order of Monseigneur, and therefore foisted on all public employments." Although the Marquis is out of Monseigneur's favor, he is nevertheless the perfect aristocrat: he can respond to others only in terms of their class and recognizes no common bonds of humanity. His carriage kills a child, and he can see the event only in terms of his contempt for the poor: "I would ride over any of you very willingly, and exterminate you from the earth." To his nephew Charles Darnay, he laments the deterioration of the power of the aristocracy: "Our not remote ancestors held the right of life and death over the surrounding vulgar." The Marquis despises Darnay for his humane feelings. And of course, there are the events related in Dr. Manette's prison diary in which the Marquis and his brother destroy a peasant family. . . .

A NEW ORDER NO BETTER THAN THE OLD

If the French Revolution is a form of retribution for such distortions of humanity, it is also paradoxically a continuation of them; the new order merely perpetuates the dehumanizing class-consciousness of the old. Just as the Marquis and the society he represents were trapped within a system that

allowed them to perceive others only in terms of their position within the social system, so too are the revolutionaries
trapped within their own inversion of that system. Charles
Darnay's journey into France most clearly dramatizes how
little the overthrow of the old institutions has changed the
premises behind French society's judgments of human beings. As he prepares to leave England, Darnay comforts himself with the belief that his renunciation of his social position and his efforts to assist his impoverished tenants will
protect him; but the reader, who has seen the condemnation
of the Evrémonde race by Defarge and his fellow conspira-
tors, recognizes that Darnay's very reasonable point of view
is a misunderstanding, a projection of his own humanity
into a very inhumane situation. To the new order, Darnay
can be nothing more than the representative of a doomed
aristocratic family.

One's position as a citizen subsumes all other ties, and
revolutionary France has as little respect as the late Marquis
for the feelings that bind families together. Dr. Manette's belief that his suffering now has value as a means of saving his
son-in-law from the guillotine proves an illusion; the Revolution is unconcerned with the purely personal. The populace has revived the "questionable public virtues of antiq-
uity," so that the President of the court that is about to
condemn Darnay draws cheers from the crowd by telling Dr.
Manette "that the good physician of the Republic would deserve better still of the Republic by rooting out an obnoxious
family of Aristocrats, and would doubtless feel a sacred glow
and joy in making his daughter a widow and her child an
orphan." Madame Defarge plots to destroy the remaining
members of the Evrémonde family—Lucie, her child, and
Dr. Manette—by using their human feelings against them;
she is going to accuse them of grieving for Darnay, and in
revolutionary France even grief is subject to legal regula-
tion: mourning for a victim of the guillotine is itself a capital offense.

Dickens emphasizes the inhumanity of the French Revolution not merely for sentimental reasons but as a means of
distinguishing social upheaval from substantive change. On
the one hand, social upheaval comes about as the inevitable
result of oppression and exploitation. As the tumbrils roll
through the streets of Paris toward the guillotine, Dickens
gives a direct warning: "Crush humanity out of shape once

more, under similar hammers, and it will twist itself into the same tortured forms." On the other hand, substantive change can occur only when people discard the "mind-forg'd manacles" within which they are trapped, the state of mind that remains long after the external exploiters and oppressors have been destroyed. . . .

THE ECHOES OF CARLYLE'S VOICE

In his essay "High Victorian Literature," published in The Oxford Illustrated History of English Literature, *English scholar Andrew Sanders comments on Carlyle's influence on English society in his own day.*

Through a steady stream of essays, pamphlets, and lectures Carlyle emerged as the dominant social thinker of early Victorian England. He obliged his contemporaries to face the evident enough contradictions within their civilization and to attempt to make some sense of the disorder around them. The conflict he identified was not simply that of faith and doubt, of tradition and innovation, or of conservatism and reform, but of a gulf between the rich and the poor. . . .

Carlyle was revered as both sage and prophet by his many disciples and echoes of his voice can be heard in much of the literature of the first half of the century. In the 1840s his public protestations became all the more urgent, most notably in his lectures *On Heroes, Hero-Worship and the Heroic in History* (in which he sought new definitions of heroic action appropriate to his times) and in *Past and Present* (which bears on its title-page a quotation from Schiller expressing the vital Victorian sentiment that 'life is earnest'). *Past and Present* effectively restates the theme that had run through all of Carlyle's work to date: 'England is full of wealth, of multifarious produce, supply for human want of every kind; yet England is dying of inanition [exhaustion and emptiness].' Like the *Heroes* lectures which preceded it, the volume moves towards the idea of a hero who transcends the 'shams' and 'quackery' of the times, and whose will and action is capable of galvanizing society and forcibly moving history forward.

Without such an inner transformation, the new order in France can only perpetuate the old oppression by continuing the inherited class-based assumptions about what human beings are. For Dickens, revolution is institutional, but change is psychic. . . .

AN INDIVIDUAL SENSE OF PURPOSE

Such change has effects that are felt only within the sphere of immediate relationships. It is not the result of dedication to great causes but of following the injunction that Carlyle borrowed from [the eighteenth-century German writer Johann von] Goethe: "*Do the Duty which lies nearest thee.*" Thus Sidney Carton finds a sense of purposefulness through his devotion to Lucie to whom he has said "For you, and for any dear to you, I would do anything." Like Dr. Manette, Carton exemplifies the contradictory possibilities inherent in human nature. He has told Darnay after the courtroom scene of his sense of emotional isolation and he tells Lucie, "I am like one who died young. All my life might have been." But as he walks through Paris with his mind set on sacrificing himself to help Lucie and her family, a sense of relatedness returns; he remembers his father's funeral, and the words of the burial service pass through his mind. And his changed state appears to the very last not only in the dramatic act of dying in the place of another but also in the kindness that he displays toward the seamstress who precedes him to the guillotine. Carton's love for Lucie has aroused the sympathetic capacity within his nature, and by caring for another, he finally emerges from the self-imposed prison of indifference. He is finally able to respond to those around him.

Clearly Dickens is not giving us any formula for the regeneration of the human race; the most radical effect that individual change brings about is reconciliation within families. This emphasis on intimate relationships does imply a view of society, but that view is largely negative: the individual must not be excessively burdened by his social identity, he must have room to develop with the contradictory fullness that is distinctively human. But even within a culture that offers that possibility, society does not offer any encouragement to the best human impulses. If Doctor Manette is recalled to life from the grave of his imprisonment, John Barsad parodies that same theme in his mock funeral and reappearance in France as precisely what he has always been, a spy. If Charles Darnay uses the freedom from the past that England offers him to make a new and productive life, Sidney Carton, the character who so uncannily resembles Darnay, is too paralyzed to realize either his emotional or professional capabilities except in his final self-sacrifice.

The love of Lucie Manette acts as a regenerative force, but not all women have that power. Miss Pross maintains an unquestioning loyalty to her brother, a loyalty that has no effect other than relieving her of all her property, and Jerry Cruncher remains through most of the book insensible to his wife's prayers. Lucie is clearly a force for the good, but the French episodes, with their portrait of the bloodthirsty Madame Defarge and her companions, effectively undercut any notion that Dickens uncritically idealizes women as moral forces. In *A Tale of Two Cities*, no external circumstance can do more than create an atmosphere in which change is possible; the individual's readiness is all.

AN ACCEPTANCE OF SOCIAL DESPAIR

A Tale of Two Cities does not pose domesticity and religion as remedies for the great social problems of the nineteenth century; at most, Dickens's versions of faith and family offer the individual some refuge from the void left by the futility of public action. For whatever solutions Dickens offers are given with the same awareness that is the basis of Carlyle's social criticism: the old clothes of society—its beliefs, its institutions, its politics—are worn out and no longer fill human needs. Thus the novel's tale of private romance becomes a confession of public despair. At the end of the book, the characters retreat into domesticity only after both Darnay and Dr. Manette have tried to influence the course of public events and have clearly failed. Institutions seem impervious to human effort: good men waste their lives if they engage in activism. What Dickens can do on a miniature scale—redefine traditional institutions so that a small group can be based on human values—he cannot do for his culture. . . . Dickens recognized the death of the old world but could not visualize the birth of a new.

Certainly as so many critics have claimed, this novel leaves the reader dissatisfied, and part of that dissatisfaction is rooted in Dickens's tendency toward facile moralizing. But the novel also deliberately engenders dissatisfaction through its presentation of the extreme disparity between public and private life. Institutions exist not only as social mechanisms but also through the states of mind they create within their culture, and to destroy the mechanisms cannot in itself bring about substantive change. The old order in France had created a society of unidimensional men who in the overthrow of the past could not break away from the enslaving spirit of their history. The French Revolution abolishes the monarchy, abolishes the aristocracy, abolishes the financial exploiters, but in its perverse way, it embodies the values of these traditional oppressors.

The malaise that Dickens sees in the French Revolution is characteristic of his anatomy of society in his late novels. *A Tale of Two Cities* presents in its most extreme form the same inability to translate private virtue into public action that in other novels plagues English society; the Circumlocution Office in *Little Dorrit* and the Court of Chancery in *Bleak House* poison the will of Englishmen. These institutions work according to their own internal logic and not to fulfill any human need.... They dehumanize anyone who comes into contact with them. Such institutions respond to nothing outside of themselves. It is better, Dickens says, to retreat into a sphere of a few close relationships where action becomes meaningful, to make one's garden grow; but whatever hope Dickens offers for private life grows out of an acceptance of social despair.

Unlike Dickens, Carlyle seems to offer some hope that the process by which men change themselves and dedicate their energies to the fulfillment of their immediate duties can perhaps in the long run transform society. It is likely that this hope struck a responsive note in his contemporaries and brought Carlyle to the height of his popularity in the late 1830s and the 1840s. It is also probably the extinction of that hope that brought to the fore Carlyle's more authoritarian tendencies and that to some degree alienated him from a part of his audience. But the differences between Carlyle and Dickens should not obscure the basic similarity of their outlooks: both writers believe that man's self-realization can occur only in a social context and yet that contact with society is inherently destructive.... Both Carlyle and Dickens are seeking a means by which people can experience a sense of purposeful action in a society whose institutions are devoid of all human purpose and whose populace has come to reflect that inhumanity.

Generational Conflict in Dickens's *Tale*

Albert D. Hutter

In his version of the French Revolution, Dickens portrayed not only a nation suddenly in conflict with its own past traditions, but also generations of individual families within that nation struggling to cope with and ultimately to break away from the actions of those who preceded them. In this essay, scholar Albert D. Hutter of the University of California, Los Angeles, suggests that in this Dickens novel the sins of the fathers are constantly repeated, eventually leading to generational conflict that mirrors the national political conflict of the turbulent times. One way the synthesis of nation and generation is symbolized, says Hutter, is in Charles Darnay's struggle with three different father figures: his own father, his father's twin, and his father-in-law. But this struggle is overshadowed by the larger sins of the nation, which, in the form of revolutionary terror, lead to still more sin. And all the while, images of parents killing children and children killing parents are constantly repeated in the story. Hutter concludes that Dickens used Sydney Carton's Christ-like act of sacrifice in the finale as a way of finally breaking the cycle of repeated generational conflict.

Two revolutions, one generational and the other political, determine the structure of *A Tale of Two Cities*. We require a combination of critical methods—literary, psychoanalytic, historical—to illuminate the novel's complex structure and its impact on different readers. [Literary scholar] Lee Sterrenburg writes that Dickens' vision of the French Revolution may be influenced by "a personal daydream only he can fully fathom. But he is able to communicate with his

Reprinted by permission of The Modern Language Association of America from "Nation and Generation in *A Tale of Two Cities*" by Albert D. Hutter, *PMLA*, vol. 93, no. 3, May 1978, pp. 448-58.

readers because he has rendered his daydream in terms of a publicly meaningful iconography [symbolism]." Since *A Tale of Two Cities* is also a tale of two generations, the iconography of father-son conflict carries a particularly powerful social resonance.

Dickens' novel was published in 1859, a year that Asa Briggs [author of *Victorian People*] calls a "turning point" in the "late Victorian revolt against authority." This revolt originated "in mid-Victorian society. What happened inside families then influenced what happened in many areas of public life later." The major publications of 1859, from *The Origin of Species* and Marx's *Critique of Political Economy* to Samuel Smiles's *Self-Help*, stand poised between the anticipation of a later ideological revolt and the still-powerful memory of the French Revolution. That revolution and subsequent English social reform inevitably changed Victorian father-son relations. But the changing Victorian family, in turn, reshaped society. As much as any other work of 1859, *A Tale of Two Cities* demonstrates the correlation between family and nation, and it uses the language of psychological conflict and psychological identification to portray social upheaval and the restoration of social order.

DR. MANETTE'S TRAUMA

Nation and generation converge in the earliest chronological event of *A Tale of Two Cities*, Doctor Manette's story of the Evrémondes' brutality (III, 10). The Evrémondes rape a young peasant girl, wound her brother, then summon Manette to treat their victims. When Manette tries to report these crimes, he is incarcerated in the Bastille. He writes a full account of his experience—damning the Evrémondes to the last of their race—and hides this personal history in his cell. Defarge finds the document and uses it as evidence against Charles Darnay, né Evrémonde. The events Manette describes, a microcosm of the larger narrative, trigger the major actions and reversals of the double plot. The rape itself implies social exploitation. . . . Conversely, one peasant's attack on his master anticipates the nation's reply to such abuse. The Evrémonde who raped the girl and murdered her brother will later run down a small child from the Paris slums, and as a result will be "driven fast to his tomb." The retaliation denied one peasant, a generation earlier, is carried out by the revolutionary "Jacques." Even the Paris tri-

bunal at which Manette's story is read reflects a struggle between parents and children: Manette has condemned his
son-in-law to death.

Class conflict here reveals a hidden psychological conflict
that recurs throughout the novel. Manette is taken at night
and forced to witness the aftermath of a violent sexual assault. His abductors have absolute power, and any knowledge of their activities carries grave risk: "The things that you
see here," the Marquis warns young Manette, "are things to
be seen, and not spoken of" (III, 10). Violence and sexuality,
combined with a mysterious nocturnal setting and a dangerous observation, suggest a primal scene. Such scenes arouse
anxiety about being caught spying, and they invariably reflect parent-child conflict. The political significance of this
drama intensifies its psychological meaning. Evrémonde's
absolute power, for example, resembles the father's absolute
power over his child. The novel's virtual obsession with spying, its comic subplot, and its descriptions of revolutionary
violence all further suggest primal-scene fantasies. . . .

Manette's story is the narrative equivalent of a trauma: it
recalls an event that precedes all the other action of the
novel and organizes that action, although it is not "recovered" until quite late in the novel. Modern psychoanalytic
theory recognizes. the retrospective quality of trauma, the
way in which the individual reconstructs his past life to con-
form with present conflicts and thereby invests a past event
with significance—some of it real, often some of it imagined.
Manette's document stands in a similar relationship to the
larger novel: within the structure of the *Tale* it acts like a
traumatic memory, reliving the significant antecedent
events of the entire plot at the climax of Darnay's second
trial. The document reveals the combination of public and
private acts that informs the narrative; it records the "primal
scene" of the text itself.

Because Dickens makes this document the hidden nexus
of the plot, it must bear a considerable weight of coincidence. The abused peasants are the brother and sister of
Madame Defarge; Ernest Defarge was originally Doctor
Manette's servant; and Manette, before being rushed off to
the Bastille, even meets his future son-in-law. Manette is
sought out by the Marquise St. Evrémonde, who has "a pre-
sentiment that if no other innocent atonement is made" for
the wrongdoing of her husband and brother-in-law, "it will

one day be required" of little Charles (III, 10)—a prophecy
as remarkable as any of the "spiritual revelations" satirized
by Dickens in the first chapter.

FILLED WITH SPIES AND MURDERERS

Like the story of Doctor Manette, the larger action of the
novel turns on seeing what was never meant to be seen, an
experience symbolized by the extensive use of a "Gorgon's
Head." This mythical figure, which turned those who looked
at it into stone, is now itself a "stone face [which] seemed to
stare amazed, and, with opened mouth and dropped under-
jaw, looked awe-stricken" (II, 9). The novel begins by opposing things hidden and things revealed. The passengers
on the Dover Mail "were wrapped to the cheek-bones and
over the ears, and wore jack-boots. Not one of the three
could have said, from anything he saw, what either of the
other two was like; and each was hidden under almost as
many wrappers from the eyes of the mind, as from the eyes
of the body, of his two companions" (I, 2). And we are repeatedly aware of eyes, hundreds of eyes, at critical moments in the text, such as Darnay's appearance at his London trial:

> Everybody present . . . stared at him. . . . Eager faces strained
> round pillars and corners, to get a sight of him; spectators in
> back rows stood up, not to miss a hair of him; people on the
> floor of the court, laid their hands on the shoulders of the
> people before them, to help themselves, at anybody's cost, to
> a view of him—stood a-tiptoe, got upon ledges, stood upon
> next to nothing, to see every inch of him.   ("A Sight"—II, 2)

At Darnay's second Paris trial, Dickens halts the action by a
momentary frieze of staring spectators:

> In a dead silence and stillness—the prisoner under trial look-
> ing lovingly at his wife, his wife only looking from him to
> look with solicitude at her father, Doctor Manette keeping his
> eyes fixed on the reader, Madame Defarge never taking hers
> from the prisoner, Defarge never taking his from his feasting
> wife, and all the other eyes there intent upon the Doctor, who
> saw none of them—the paper was read, as follows.   (III, 9)

The novel is filled with spies, from a hero twice accused of
spying, to the comic spying of Jerry Cruncher, Jr., on his father, to the spy Barsad and "the great brotherhood of Spies"
(II, 22) who inhabit St. Antoine. Even the dead men, their
heads on Temple Bar, remind us of "the horror of being
ogled" (II, 1). And the novel closes with an obsessive parade

of violence, the revolutionaries worshiping the guillotine and previewing its victims at mass trials.

Spying, like virtually everything else in this novel, has two meanings—one public, the other private. The official spies, like Barsad, are instruments of repression and representatives of the "fathers," the men in power. But in other contexts, like the Cruncher scenes, children spy on their parents. In both cases spying expresses the *Tale*'s dominant conflicts. Thus the Gorgon's Head witnesses much more than the murder of the Marquis: it sees the deadly struggle between two generations, which is climaxed by implicit filicide [killing of a son or daughter] and patricide. . . .

The Marquis has desired the death of his nephew, and Charles, more covertly, has imagined the sudden death of his father's twin. There is the suggestion, but never the realization, of both filicide and patricide. But the exchange between the Marquis and his nephew is framed by the murder of a child and the murder of the Marquis himself. The former symbolizes the Marquis's murderous impulses toward his brother's child, as well as the cruelty of the French ruling classes toward their dependents, like the abuse witnessed by Doctor Manette eighteen years earlier. At the same time, the revenge that follows is both an actualization of Charles's revenge against his father's surrogate and a gesture that shows the French peasantry rising up to murder its rulers, as they will ultimately murder the father of their country in the revolutionary act of regicide. Dickens clarifies these connections when he describes the rumors that follow the capture of the Marquis's assassin:

> . . . he is brought down into our country to be executed on the spot, and . . . he will very certainly be executed. They even whisper that because he has slain Monseigneur, and because Monseigneur was the father of his tenants—serfs—what you will—he will be executed as a parricide . . . his right hand, armed with the knife, will be burnt off before his face . . . into wounds which will be made in his arms, his breast, and his legs, there will be poured boiling oil, melted lead, hot resin, wax, and sulphur; finally . . . he will be torn limb from limb by four strong horses.   (II, 15)

That Darnay should flee such a country is hardly surprising, but the political reasons for flight are intensified by his personal desire to avoid the retribution prophesied by his mother for the sins of his fathers. And the futility of that flight becomes apparent with his return to France after the

Revolution. Darnay's fate is to be forced, against his conscious desire into a deadly struggle with his fathers: his own father, his father's identical twin, his father-in-law. Although Darnay and Manette learn to respect and love each other, their goodwill is repeatedly subverted by events. Charles's marriage to Lucie nearly kills Manette, and Manette's document in turn condemns Darnay to the guillotine. The characters seem to be moved by something larger than their individual desires, by the sins of a nation, which inevitably lead only to more sin, to an orgy of murder and retribution. The political meaning of these acts is intensified by a deep and persistent psychological theme, at times so perfectly merged with the political that one and the same act may be construed as personal revenge, patricide, and regicide.

SYDNEY CARTON REBORN

If the murderer of Evrémonde symbolically enacts Darnay's violence and vengeance, then Sydney Carton enacts another side of Darnay's character and pays for the hero's aggression. Carton's sacrifice is a convenient, if implausible, device to free Charles from the Bastille; it is also an attempt to solve an insoluble political dilemma. The revolutionaries justifiably overthrow their rulers, but their hatred leads to excesses that turn despised oppressor into sympathetic victim. The sins of the fathers are endlessly repeated, from generation to generation, and Dickens' unrealistic solution creates a character who, Christlike, will sacrifice himself for the sins of all mankind. But Carton's transformation from guilty scoundrel to hero also indicates a deeper, psychological transformation. This paragon of irreverence, having mocked and antagonized Mr. Lorry, now achieves a sudden closeness to the old banker. . . . For the first time in his knowledge of Carton, Lorry sees a "true feeling and respect"; once he decides to sacrifice himself, Carton becomes something like an ideal son and rediscovers his father in Lorry. . . .

He transforms his life by internalizing his father's image, using Lorry as a surrogate: his earlier aimlessness dissolves and a new mission identifies him with the most famous— and self-sacrificing—of sons. Carton begins to achieve a sense of historical and personal identity, and the novel ends with Carton reborn through his namesakes, Lucie's son and grandson. And with Carton's newfound strength and purpose, Darnay becomes "like a young child in [Carton's] hands." Unconscious, Darnay is delivered to old Manette and Lucie and carried out of France like a sleeping baby (III, 13). This sequence suggests that, as the hero's double internalizes paternal authority and willingly sacrifices himself to it, the innocent hero may be reborn. . . .

THE TECHNIQUE OF SPLITTING

Dickens' familial and political revolutions are expressed by his varied use of splitting throughout the novel, so that the theme of the work becomes as well its characteristic mode of expression. From the title through the rhetorically balanced opening paragraphs, Dickens establishes the "twoness" of everything to follow: characters are twinned and doubled and paired; the setting is doubled; the women, as we shall see, are split; the historical perspective is divided between an eighteenth-century event and its nineteenth-century apprehension. "Splitting" thus describes a variety of stylistic devices, particularly related to character development and plot. . . .

[For instance,] Carton's role, both as a "double" to the hero and as a melodramatic scapegoat at the close, develops the dual conflicts of the novel; indeed, much of the sentimentality of Carton-as-Christ is derived from his conversion, via Lorry, into the good son and the good conservative. Carton's solution is that of any son—or class—that willingly accepts the pain or injustice inflicted upon it by parents or rulers, and such a solution is not particularly satisfying to most readers. In his peculiarly calm and heroic way, Carton stands for the ideals of conservative belief, in the family and the nation, but he finally assumes too many meanings and is required to connect too many threads of the novel. He suffers chronically from meaning too much in relation to too many other characters and themes and, like Manette's document, unites too many incidents; he becomes more strained as he becomes more important.

Other kinds of splitting in *A Tale of Two Cities* far more successfully project the text's central conflicts, precisely because they require no resolution. Dickens' caricature of the lion and the jackal, for example, exploits an inherent, unresolvable tension in his social subject. The division of labor between Carton and Stryver powerfully suggests not only Carton's divided self but the divided goals and morals of Victorian business. . . .

A Tale of Two Cities reflects the Victorian repudiation of sexual or powerful women by contrasting the dull but idealized heroine and her more dangerous, sexual counterpart. Madame Defarge is an almost mythically frightening woman with male strength, but she has as well an animal-like beauty:

> ... [a] beauty which ... impart[s] to its possessor firmness and animosity ... a tigress. ...
>
> Such a heart Madame Defarge carried under her rough robe. Carelessly worn, it was a becoming robe enough, in a certain weird way, and her dark hair looked rich under her coarse red cap. Lying hidden in her bosom, was a loaded pistol. Lying hidden at her waist, was a sharpened dagger. Thus accoutred, and walking with the confident tread of such a character, and with the supple freedom of a woman who had habitually walked in her girlhood, barefoot and bare-legged, on the brown sea-sand, Madame Defarge took her way along the streets.   (III, 14)

Many subsequent versions of Madame Defarge, in film and in illustration, have made her a witch. The Harper and Row cover to *A Tale of Two Cities*, for example, shows a cadaverous old crone, gray-haired, hunched over her knitting, with wrinkles stitched across a tightened face. The original "Phiz" illustration, however, brings out Madame Defarge's beauty, her dark hair and her "supple freedom"; if we compare this with two later illustrations of Lucie, we realize that Madame Defarge is a strong, dark-haired version of the heroine. Characteristically, Dickens gives the Frenchwomen vitality conveyed negatively as animality ("tigress"), and denies his heroine these qualities. ...

Lucie, by contrast, is the perfect Victorian female, the ideal home companion, a loving stereotype. She achieves blandness by playing *both* child and mother (and largely skipping anything in between), so that she is all things to all generations. Darnay acknowledges that Lucie's love for her father is "an affection so unusual, so touching ... that it can have few parallels":

> "When she is clinging to you, the hands of baby, girl, and woman, all in one, are round your neck ... in loving you she sees and loves her mother at her own age, sees and loves you at my age, loves her mother brokenhearted, loves you through your dreadful trial and in your blessed restoration. I have known this, night and day, since I have known you in your home."
>
> Her father sat silent, with his face bent down.   (II, 10)

Most readers, unfortunately, do the same. . . .

This essay tries to show . . . that in *A Tale of Two Cities* Dickens is concerned with two connected themes that preoccupied him throughout his career: the generational and political conflicts he repeatedly expressed through the technique of splitting. However, because that technique is used so pervasively in *A Tale of Two Cities*, it makes the novel seem uncharacteristically concentrated in style and, at times, uncharacteristically strained or humorless. The novel's particular combination of individual psychology and broad social concerns thus accounts for its unique qualities, its intensity, and its failures. *A Tale of Two Cities* dramatizes two dominant conflicts of the Victorian age—and of our own.

The Social Collective Versus the Individual in *A Tale of Two Cities*

Cates Baldridge

Dickens lived during the height of the Victorian era in England, when most people accepted the idea that diversity and individuality were beneficial and good and, therefore, that the individual was the basic unit of society; in contrast, in revolutionary France the social collective—that is, the larger group, class, community, or polity of the "people"—was perceived to be the basic and most important social unit. This is the kernel of the argument advanced in the following essay by scholar Cates Baldridge, an assistant professor of English at Middlebury College. According to Baldridge, Dickens utilized the philosophy and imagery of the collective in *A Tale of Two Cities* partly to highlight the aggressive individualism of his own society. In a detailed analysis of Sydney Carton's role in the novel, Baldridge asserts that Dickens's depiction of Carton's highly individualistic act of heroism in the climactic scene shows that the author sympathized with the rights of the individual rather than of the collective.

Dickens's ambivalence toward the Revolution he depicts in *A Tale of Two Cities* has been the subject of much thoughtful comment, and over the past few decades a number of differing causes for this ambivalence have been proposed. [Literary scholar] George Woodcock, for instance, sees in the "vigor" with which the author depicts the scenes of Revolutionary violence a kind of vicarious retribution against the society which betrayed him in his youth: "in one self [Dickens] is there, dancing among them, destroying prisons and

Excerpted from "Alternatives to Bourgeois Individualism in *A Tale of Two Cities*" by Cates Baldridge, *SEL: Studies in English Literature, 1500-1900*, vol. 30, no. 4 (Autumn 1990). Reprinted by permission of *SEL*.

taking revenge for the injustices of childhood." Others have interpreted it as the result of the author's fitful attempts to work out an overarching theory of history, or to adapt Carlyle's ideas on historical necessity to the needs of his fictional genre. . . . What I shall do here is to focus upon one particular aspect of the Revolutionary regime in *A Tale* which has received less attention than most, and attempt to put forward a largely political explanation for Dickens's ambivalence concerning it. The aspect I refer to is the Revolution's assertion that the group, the class, the Republic—and *not* the individual—comprise, or should comprise, the basic unit of society. The corollaries which spring from this belief (and which are themselves fully depicted in the text) will also be considered: that all merely personal claims must defer to those of the polity as a whole; that the minds and hearts of citizens must be laid bare to the scrutiny of the community; and that virtues and guilt, rights and responsibilities, inhere in groups rather than in individuals. My contention is that Dickens's deep dissatisfaction with the social relations fostered by his own acquisitive and aggressively individualist society leads him at times to explore with sensitivity and even enthusiasm the liberating possibilities offered by an ideology centered elsewhere than upon the autonomous self. As we shall see, what emerges is a subversive subtext to the narrator's middle-class horror at the collectivist Revolutionary ideology promulgated behind the barricades of Paris. . . .

THE MIDDLE-CLASS INDIVIDUAL

Clearly, we should not expect any such countervailing current of thought as the one outlined above to emerge except in thoroughly disguised and displaced forms, for . . . the assumptions of bourgeois [middle-class] individualism are central to the enterprise of Victorian novelists generally and to that of Dickens in particular. Middle-class orthodoxy posits the discrete human subject as primary and inviolable, a move which . . . [lies at the] core of Classical Liberalism. . . . Broadly defined, Liberalism is, says [author of *Character and the Novel*, W.J.] Harvey, a "state of mind [which] has as its controlling centre an acknowledgment of the plenitude, diversity and individuality of human beings in society, together with the belief that such characteristics are good as ends in themselves," and he goes on to assert that "tolerance, skepticism, [and] respect for the autonomy of others are its watchwords" while "fanaticism and the monolithic creed [are] its abhorrence." Harvey's phrasing may strike some as overly laudatory, but it does help to underscore why the chronically permeable barriers of the self in *A Tale of Two Cities* constitute such a politically dangerous issue: in depicting the Revolution, the text takes pains to portray—and to roundly denounce—a counterideology to Classical Liberalism, in which the claims of the individual are assumed to be secondary to those of the collectivity, and in which the individual is seen as anything but sacrosanct. It should come as little surprise, then, that Dickens's most forceful statement of subversive sympathy for the Revolution's attack upon the idea of the discrete subject, his most anguished confession of ambivalence concerning the bourgeois notion of an inviolable individual, comprises what has long been considered merely an "anomalous" or "digressive" portion of the text—I refer specifically to the "Night Shadows" passage, a striking meditation upon the impenetrable barriers separating man from man which has proved perennially troublesome to readers.

> A wonderful fact to reflect upon, that every human creature is constituted to be that profound secret and mystery to every other. A solemn consideration, when I enter a great city by night, that every one of those darkly clustered houses encloses its own secret; that every room in every one of them encloses its own secret; that every beating heart in the hundreds of thousands of breasts there, is, in some of its imaginings, a secret to the heart nearest it! Something of the awfulness, even of Death itself, is referable to this. No more can I turn the leaves of this dear book that I loved, and vainly hope in time to read it all. No more can I look into the depths of this unfathomable water, wherein, as momentary lights glanced into it, I have had glimpses of buried treasure and other things submerged. It was appointed that the book should shut with a spring, for ever and for ever, when I had read but a page. It was appointed that the water should be locked in an eternal frost, when the light was playing on its surface, and I stood in ignorance on the shore. My friend is dead, my neighbour is dead, my love, the darling of my soul, is dead; it is the inexorable consolidation and perpetuation of the secret that was always in that individuality, and which I shall carry in mine to my life's end. In any of the burial-places of this city through which I pass, is there a sleeper more inscrutable than its busy inhabitants are, in their innermost personality, to me, or than I am to them?

The relationship of this passage to the major concerns of the novel has struck many a critic as problematic. Some have sought to link it with the rest of the text merely by pointing out its similarities to Carlyle's practice of dramatizing the miraculous hidden within the mundane, and thus to account for it as yet another example of the literary influence of Dickens's occasional mentor. . . .

I believe that there is in fact a broadly thematic resonance to the passage—a resonance which is crucial to the book's attitudes concerning bourgeois individualism and its supposedly detested alternatives. To begin with, it is significant that all the . . . critics, whatever their varying degrees of bafflement or insight, call attention to the passage's tone, for it is that aspect of the "digression" which, I believe, can most quickly lead us into its involvement with the novel's political contradictions. While the adjectives used to describe this supposed fact concerning contemporary social relations are not explicitly derogatory, the atmosphere of the paragraph as a whole is distinctly—nay, poignantly—that of a lament. What clearly comes across is a deeply felt sadness and frustration before the impermeableness of the barriers between self and self. . . . Reflecting upon the iron-clad separation of souls within the "great city" may indeed provoke wonder and awe—but it also clearly elicits a wish that things might be otherwise.

MADAME DEFARGE'S ROSTER OF VICTIMS

The imagery employed in the passage is also pertinent if we remember that the working title of a *Tale* was "Buried Alive," for the passage continually attempts to blur the distinction between life and death, presenting a portrait of urban existence as a kind of living entombment. Not only does the incommunicability of souls have "something of the awfulness, even of Death itself . . . referable" to it, but the narrator, in his quest for closer communion with his fellow beings, speaks of himself as looking into "depths" for "glimpses of buried treasure." Furthermore, the deaths of his friend, neighbor, and love are described as "the inexorable consolidation and perpetuation" of their isolated, living states—as if these people are most true to their nature only after they have ceased to breathe. The final sentence, in which the corpses in actual graveyards are declared to be "sleepers" no more "inscrutable" than the town's "busy inhabitants," completes the equation of the living community with that of the dead. What the narrator has accomplished here is graphically to portray the "great city" as a metropolis in which everyone is virtually "buried alive": to depict a condition of society in which each citizen goes about his everyday offices—and even endures his supposedly most intimate moments—enclosed in a sarcophagus of impenetrable individuality. As we shall see, this damning critique of the way we live now inaugurates the subversive subtext which runs beside and beneath the narrator's subsequent denigration of the French Revolution's insistence that collectivities must supersede the individual as the fundamental unit of social life; it is here that we can apprehend the first movement of that counter-current which dares to consider the ideology of the Jacquerie as a possible escape from the "solitary confinement" mandated by bourgeois individualism. . . .

At the storming of the Bastille, for instance, we get the following call to arms, ostensibly from Defarge: "Work, comrades all, work! Work, Jacques One, Jacques Two, Jacques One Thousand, Jacques Two Thousand, Jacques Five-and-Twenty Thousand; in the name of all the Angels or the Devils—which you prefer—work!" And, as with Monsieur Defarge's lieutenants, so with Madame's, for it has been noted that "The Vengeance" is one of several nicknames indicative of "the tendency toward generalization and abstraction" in the novel. This "tendency," given the political concerns of *A Tale*, becomes highly subversive, for in a world of merely generic entities, the discriminations upon which bourgeois law and political economy depend simply cannot be made— the idea that "we are all equally guilty" is anathema [loathsome] to Victorian orthodoxy.

This brings us, of course, to Madame Defarge's attitudes concerning who deserves to suffer for the sins of the Ancien Regime, for these constitute the most sinister instance of moral collectivism the novel has to offer. When Darnay is arrested and flung into prison his defense rests upon his assertion that he is not *personally* responsible for the crimes either of the aristocracy in general or of his family in particular. This argument carries no weight with Madame, however, for her mind is simply incapable of focusing upon any moral entity so small and discrete as an individual—her roster of victims and villains being filled exclusively with the names of groups. Speaking of the Evrémondes, she says that "for other crimes as tyrants and oppressors [she has] this *race* a long time on [her] register, doomed to destruction and extermination." Halting the slaughter at those who can claim innocence only for themselves and not their class strikes her as unsound:

> "It is true what madame says," observed Jacques Three. "Why stop? There is great force in that. Why stop?"
> "Well, well," reasoned [Monsieur] Defarge, "but one must stop somewhere. After all, the question is still where?"
> "At extermination," said Madame.
> "Magnificent!" croaked Jacques Three. The Vengeance, also, highly approved.

Lucie—apparently intuiting the bent of Madame's mind in the heat of distress—appeals to her for mercy as a "sister-woman" as well as a wife and mother, but this bit of rhetoric, meant to mask a personal appeal in collectivist diction, fails to take in Madame Defarge: "We have borne this a long time. . . . Is it likely that the trouble of one wife and mother would be much to us now?" As Madame makes her way through the streets on her way to kill Lucie and the child, the narrator sums up that blind spot in her moral vision which the champion of bourgeois individualism cannot help but abhor: "It was nothing to her, that an innocent man was to die for the sins of his forefathers; she saw, not him, but them.". . .

SYDNEY CARTON'S OPAQUE CHARACTER

I will now turn from *A Tale of Two Cities*'s explicit rhetoric to its countervailing subtext and examine those passages in which the novel's repressed desire to escape the constraints of its own prevailing ideology can best be discerned. My argument is that the sentiments voiced in the "anomalous" Night Shadows passage do in fact recur throughout the text, but that Dickens's sincere allegiance to the commonplaces of Classical Liberalism forces him to displace them in two directions: toward the comic and toward the private. The former movement is expressed through Jarvis Lorry's at best intermittently successful suppression of his own personal claims in the interest of Tellson's Bank, a process which is rendered yet more innocuous by that institution's exaggerated traditionalism and firm allegiance to bourgeois social practices. . . . The latter—and more important—movement manifests itself in the trajectory of Sydney Carton's career. As we shall see, Carton's progress through the text first underscores the pernicious effects of bourgeois-capitalist concep-

tions of individualism, then affirms the heroic potential unleashed by abandoning them, only to turn back upon itself
and to reaffirm the tenets of Classical Liberalism in its last
hours. Furthermore, Carton is allowed to escape the cultur-
ally dictated bounds of the self only in a manner which ob-
fuscates the process's ideological import: for a few crucial
moments he and Darnay genuinely transcend those traditional barriers which wall off the inviolable individual from
all his fellow beings, but this merging of a *single* discrete self
with *one* other deflects a broad social goal of the Revolution
into the realm of private psychology—and then too, it is performed as part of an attempt to *thwart* the very Revolutionary practices it imitates in miniature. . . .

When we first encounter Sydney, he appears to be the
very embodiment of the secretive and unfathomable individual lamented in the Night Shadows passage. Darnay, his
outward double, feels as if he is in "a dream" in his presence,
and indeed no one else—not Lorry, certainly, or even
Stryver—has much of a clue as to what he is really about.
The political implications of Carton's opaque character
come to the fore as soon as we recall the work he performs,
for as Stryver's "jackal" he enacts what can almost be
termed a parody of the division of labor which upholds
bourgeois capitalism. He and Stryver, it should be remembered, divide between them what should rightly be the labor
of a single person, and furthermore, this "division" is anything but equitable—Carton performs the labor, Stryver gar-
ners the credit. Moreover, the very nicknames "jackal" and
"lion" seem to replicate the social practices of Victorian society at large, heaping opprobrium [disgrace] upon the faceless who sell their labor, lauding the famous who purchase
it. . . . Carton, then, though distinctly odd, is in a real sense a
typical citizen of Dickens's nocturnal city of unknowable individuals the victim of alienated labor, he too is "buried
alive." Thus, if we now recall Lorry's attitude toward his
"business" at Tellson's—so fraught with Revolutionary con-
notations—and contrast them with Carton's view of his own
labors, the following exchange between Sydney and the
banker takes on a new significance:

> "And indeed, sir," pursued Mr. Lorry, not minding him, "I
> really don't know what you have to do with the matter. If
> you'll excuse me, as very much your elder, for saying so, I re-
> ally don't know that it is your business."

> "Business! Bless you, *I* have no business," said Mr. Carton.
> "It is a pity you have not, sir."
> "I think so too."
> "If you had," pursued Mr. Lorry, "perhaps you would at-
> tend to it."
> "Lord love you, no!—I shouldn't," said Mr. Carton.

Carton possesses "no business" and further confesses that he
has always "fallen into" his proper "rank," which he describes as "nowhere." Now, since in Lorry's case it is precisely "doing business" which beneficently makes him as
one with the collectivity of the House, Carton's having *no*
business can be taken as yet another marker of his perverse
(but socially endemic) isolation from all larger communities,
an isolation which renders his life and labor meaningless. . . .

Carton Absorbed into a Larger Entity

As it happens, Sydney does eventually puncture the . . . walls
which close him off from the world. . . . This is accomplished through his remarkable commingling with Darnay
on the eve of his execution, an escape from the constraints
of bourgeois individualism which is prepared for by the fact
that Carton and Darnay bear a strong physical resemblance
to each other. . . .

The central irony which emerges from Carton's successful commingling with Darnay in prison is that Sydney's
"cure" is effected in the shadow of the novel's explicit condemnation of the very practice which heals him, for while he
participates in a process whereby one man is able to transcend the suffocating barriers of the bourgeois self, the Revolution's insistence that the same is to be done for *all* men
meets with nothing but scorn. And here one can anticipate
an objection: the obvious fact that Sydney and the Jacquerie
see the annihilation of the conventional barriers between individuals as the means to ends which are diametrically opposed does not weaken this irony to the extent that one might
initially suppose. Yes, Carton abandons his personal claims
for the protection of bourgeois domesticity (one might even
say for the Victorian hearth, since Sydney's figurative descendants are to recount his story for generations) while the
Paris Tribunal demands that the individual subsume himself
into the polity in order to speed the flourishing of, as the narrator puts it, the Republic One and Indivisible of Liberty,
Equality, Fraternity, or Death. But my point is that the former
cause rests upon the foundation stone of bourgeois individ-

ualism while the latter is committed to its destruction, and that Carton can only ensure the safety of Liberal society (in the form of the Darnays, Manette, Lorry, and Pross) by temporarily violating one of its fundamental tenets. To put it another way, Carton can only make the world safe for discrete subjects by temporarily ceasing to be one himself and thereby blocking the plans of a regime bent on abolishing the entire concept of the discrete subject forevermore. . . .

As Sydney takes his famous midnight walk the night before the second Parisian trial, his steps are dogged by religious images, and he repeats "I am the resurrection and the life" continually to himself as he wanders. At one point, though, he pauses to sleep, and, in a moment obviously fraught with symbolic meaning, awakes to find an analogue of his life in the motions of the Seine [River]:

> The strong tide, so swift, so deep, and certain, was like a congenial friend, in the morning stillness. He walked by the stream, far from the houses, and in the light and warmth of the sun fell asleep on the bank. When he awoke and was afoot again, he lingered there yet a little longer, watching an eddy that turned and turned purposeless, until the stream absorbed it, and carried it on to the sea.—"Like me!"

When one considers that Sydney has resolved to sacrifice himself in order to thwart the collectivist wrath of the Revolution, this passage reads curiously indeed, for cutting across the obvious message concerning Carton's lassitude giving way to action, there is the further hint that to do so involves subsuming himself in a larger entity. One could perhaps suggest that he is being "absorbed" into the greater life of humanity at large or into the Christian dispensation were it not for the quite programmatic way in which "tide," and "sea" have been associated throughout *A Tale* with the Revolutionary mob. The "strong tide, so swift, so deep, and certain" which now appears as Carton's "congenial friend" and into which his life is "absorbed" may not partake of the violence of that which breaks against the Bastille, but the provocative choice of simile cannot help but alert us to a parallel between Sydney's path to personal salvation and the Revolution's recipe for a secular utopia beyond the constraints of bourgeois individualism. . . .

ONLY INDIVIDUALS MAY HAUNT THE LIVING

That Dickens was aware at some level of the parallels he had drawn can be deduced from the violent reaction which occurs in the novel's final pages, for there he takes pains to insist that although Carton is in one sense just another face among a crowd of the condemned—one more victim of what is essentially a mass murder—he nevertheless stands out as a distinct individual whose personality will remain intact even beyond the grave. This reaction begins as the narrator follows his protagonist from cell to guillotine. After emphasizing that the prison officials are exclusively concerned about the "count" in the tumbrils—that there be fifty-two bodies in it—he goes on to provide us with a catalogue of the condemned's deportment which makes it clear that they are all quite discrete personalities:

> Of the riders in the tumbrils, some observe these things, and all things on their last roadside, with an impassive stare; others, with a lingering interest in the ways of life and men. Some, seated with drooping heads, are sunk in silent despair; again, there are some so heedful of their looks that they cast upon the multitude such glances as they have seen in theatres, and in pictures. Several close their eyes, and think, or try to get their straying thoughts together. Only one, and he a miserable creature, of a crazed aspect, is so shattered and made drunk by horror, that he sings, and tries to dance.

Carton's own possibly "prophetic" speech at the foot of the scaffold gives us a taste of individualism triumphant, with Sydney personally persisting through the generations. He sees Lucie "with a child upon her bosom, who bears [his] name," a child who eventually "win[s] his way up in that path of life which once was [his]" and who in turn fathers a "boy of [Carton's] name," to whom he "tell[s] . . . [Sydney's] story, with a tender and faltering voice.". . . Indeed, Sydney's . . . middle-class individuality seems so firmly and solidly back in place that not even the worm can worry it, and this sense of the protagonist's "haunting" both the place of his death and future generations is very much to the point, for it cancels out several passages in which the Revolution's practice of mass killing threatens to endorse their anti-individualist ideology by sheer weight of numbers and frequency. . . . Haunting is the individualist pursuit *par excellence*—only individuals may haunt the living, not groups or classes. And thus Carton's death—and his subsequent life after death— stridently refute the collectivist ideology, insisting as they do both upon the individual's persistent influence in secular history and hinting of the spiritual indwelling which is the religious sanction for the discrete subject of Classical Liberalism, a subject conceived of as retaining its individuality even beyond the grave. As the author of *A Tale of Two Cities* was well aware, serious contemplations concerning the obscuring walls of the bourgeois self have "something of the awfulness, even of Death" about them.... After tracing Lorry and Carton's well disguised escapes from the constricting confines of bourgeois individualism, one understands better just how secretly liberating the "doing" part of Dickens's enterprise must have seemed to him, and how truly he bespoke his deep frustration with Victorian culture in calling the era of the Revolution both the *best* and the worst of times.

Cyclical History in
A Tale of Two Cities

Elliot L. Gilbert

Most historians and scholars typically present history in a straightforward chronology. By contrast, literary scholar Elliot L. Gilbert argues that Dickens tells the events of the French Revolution in the style of Thomas Carlyle, Dickens's friend. Carlyle saw history not as an accumulation of "dead events," but as a combination of trends, actions, and mistakes that are fated to repeat themselves endlessly into the future. This cyclic vision of history philosophizes that both past and future events and personalities are, more or less, like those of the "eternal present." Gilbert points out that Dickens adopts this approach in *Tale*'s opening lines, which state that conditions in the previous century (the eighteenth) apply just as well in the present, the nineteenth century.

England also had its French Revolution, a revolution history has rather unexcitedly labeled "The First Reform Bill." Like most English versions of continental movements, this English "French Revolution" was rather belated, did not take place, in fact, until nearly half a century after its Gallic counterpart. Also like most English versions of continental movements, it was comparatively subdued. To be sure, this revolution too was preceded by acts of violence—by riots, machine-breaking, rick-burning, tax strikes, and other demonstrations—but these stopped well short of the wholesale insurrectionary destructiveness of the 1789 rebellion across the channel. Indeed, the First Reform Bill, as its name implies, was a constitutional revolution, one that even included a typically English comic opera plot twist that . . . gives a wry new meaning to the phrase "a tale of two cities." For where the people of Paris, with characteristic rational-

Excerpted from "'To Awake from History': Carlyle, Thackeray, and *A Tale of Two Cities*" by Elliot L. Gilbert, *Dickens Studies Annual*, vol. 12 (1983), pp. 247-64. Reprinted by permission of AMS Press, New York, N.Y.

ism and directness, undertook to destroy the power of their aristocrats by bloodily reducing their number, the government in London succeeded in curtailing the power of the House of Lords, which had voted against the Reform Bill, by threatening to create so many new lords favorable to the bill that the legislation would be sure to pass. And in fact, such an important political, economic, and social watershed was this revolutionary act of Parliament that historians have come to date the Victorian Period not from 1837, the year Victoria ascended the throne, but rather from 1832, the year of the passage of the First Reform Bill.

DELIBERATE ATTACKS ON HISTORY

Despite their differences, these French and English revolutions had several striking similarities. First, they were both efforts to shift the balance of political power in their countries, to take authority away from those who exercised it by virtue of hereditary right and to give it instead to those who had earned it more or less through their own achievements. For decades during the late eighteenth and early nineteenth centuries, the real economic power of the state had come more and more to be controlled by entrepreneurial capitalists, by self-made "captains of industry," to use [historian Thomas] Carlyle's famous phrase, while the political power of the state remained in the hands of men whose only claim to it was that they had been fortunate in their genealogies, that, like their fathers and grandfathers before them, they were inheritors of land. Eventually, however, the gulf between real and traditional power in these nations grew so great that it could no longer be denied or minimized, and at that point a correction of the imbalance occurred, in France through regicide [murder of kings and queens] and the Terror, in England by a widening of the franchise.

A second similarity between the French and English revolutions, one growing out of the first but moving dramatically beyond it, was that both the 1789 rebellion and the 1832 legislation constituted massive and deliberate attacks on history. I am speaking more than metaphorically here, for the French Revolution in particular had as one of its most conscious intentions a literal rejection of the past, a denial of the right of history to influence the present. Regicide is, of course, an obvious assault on genealogy, on the authority of the past, but just as significant were new laws restricting the right to make wills and abolishing the distinction between legitimate and natural children, and revolutionary calendar reforms establishing, among other things, the autumn equinox of 1792 as the beginning of a new chronology. For its part, the First Reform Bill, though more moderate in its methods and more figurative than literal in its language, was quite as vigorous as the French Revolution in its assault on the power of history, in its rejection of the idea that the forms and records of the past should be allowed to control the energies of the present. . . . It was especially the idea of judging history "by truth of correspondence," of trusting the historical record to bear a one-to-one relationship to some absolute reality, that began to be questioned during this period. But deprived of the authority of such correspondence, the historical record became just another literary text, one that reflected much more accurately the personal preoccupations of its writer than any nominal subject matter. . . .

We have ourselves seen a striking example of the manipulative and retroactive nature of the historical imagination. I have spoken several times thus far of what, already in the nineteenth century, historians had come to call the First Reform Bill. But it must be obvious that this could not have been the name by which this bill was originally known, since it was not until some thirty-five years later that there was a Second Reform Bill. For historians, then, to call the 1832 measure the First Reform Bill, even for the sake of making a retroactive comment about its relationship to the later event, is to misrepresent the experience of those who actually framed, debated, and voted on what for them was a unique piece of legislation. (Similarly, for history to call the 1914–1918 war "World War I" is to falsify the real experience of participants who after all thought of the conflict as "the war to end all wars.") Even more manipulative is the dating of the Victorian Period from a time five years prior to the accession of Victoria. Nothing could more clearly reveal the extent to which history, for all its aspirations to objective, scientific truth, in fact approaches to the condition of imaginative literature.

It was such a perception that helped make possible the nineteenth-century attack on history, an attack that was, like the French Revolution and the First Reform Bill, in both of which that attack was embodied, a radical assault on authority, on the authority of texts, of genealogies, of patrilineal culture; an assault, ultimately, on all efforts of the past to subvert the sovereignty and independence of the present. Certainly, this was one of the grand themes of Victorian literature. Writers of all kinds dealt with it, with the exciting potential for a new freedom and personal fulfillment that the overthrow of authority can make possible, but also with the danger of self-absorption, isolation, and silence which the absence of authority inevitably creates. And of the many books that treated this complex subject in the nineteenth century, none did so more richly or more powerfully than Charles Dickens' *A Tale of Two Cities*. . . .

A SURRENDER TO HISTORY?

Dickens begins at once to lay out those issues in *A Tale of Two Cities* with the brilliant rhetorical flourish of the opening paragraph. In a famous series of antitheses—"It was the best of times, it was the worst of times" and so on—antitheses that immediately invoke the thesis of the title, he at first seems to be trying to identify some very specific moment in history in the approved manner of the new historical science. But after he has assembled an extraordinary number of details which must infallibly, we suppose, distinguish the particular moment in question from all other, similar moments, he suddenly surprises us by announcing that these details fit the "present period" just as well as they do the previous century. In this dramatic and unexpected telescoping of two historical periods into one, Dickens adapts Carlylean anachronism [Carlyle's approach to historical writing in which he relates past and future events and personalities to the "eternal present," blurring the traditional chronological distinctions of history] to his own study of the confluence of past and present, past and present being just two more of the many contrasting but interdependent "cities" about which his tale is to be written.

The thematic statement of the opening paragraph is supported in the rest of the book by a number of images and metaphors all tending to promote the mythic and cyclical over the historical and linear. The many foreshadowings in the story, for example, help perform this function: the broken wine cask, the echoing footsteps, perhaps most memorably the evocation of the trees, already growing in the forest, that will soon be cut down and fashioned into the guillotine. In these foreshadowings, past, present, and future rush together to subvert the sovereign power of chronology.

just as the revolution itself seeks to subvert the sovereign power of genealogy. The word "Evrémonde" serves a similar anti-historical purpose in the novel. Ostensibly identifying a specific genealogical line, the name, a multilingual, two-cities pun on "everyman" or "all-the-world," and with family affiliations encompassing the full range of human behavior from the villainous to the near saintly, comes in the end to designate the whole human race.

The most ubiquitous, perhaps, of the anti-historical metaphors in the novel is that of resurrection. The first page of the book contains the phrase "recalled to life," the last page the words "I am the Resurrection and the Life," and between these two poles of the story are literally dozens of second births, from the grotesque comedy of Jerry Cruncher's body snatching, through the poignancy of the aging Jarvis Lorry traveling in a circle "nearer and nearer to the beginning," to the resonant scenes of Doctor Manette resurrected from the tomb of his prison cell, Evrémonde from the doom of his family name, Carton from the death of his soul. But resurrection, celebrating a cyclical view of existence, necessarily rejects the vision of life as a linear progress through time, in one direction only and without possibility of return, a vision that is the unavoidable first assumption of historical science. Thus, *A Tale of Two Cities* would seem to be irrevocably committed to the widespread nineteenth-century attack on history I have been examining here. . . .

Anyone who promotes an anti-historical view of life would seem to be obligated to support a revolution that itself constitutes an attack on history. Yet readers of *A Tale of Two Cities* cannot help but notice how Dickens' initial sympathy for the revolutionary figures in his book begins to wane as the story proceeds. There is, of course, one obvious practical explanation for this change of heart. We naturally sympathize more intensely with people when they are oppressed than when they themselves become oppressors, and it is just such a metamorphosis that occurs in the revolutionary group as the novel develops. But there is another, more important, issue involved here, a deeper problem that Dickens confronts in his consideration of these events and that moves him in the direction of a quite original analysis of them. . . . Dickens sees the failure of the French Revolution as deriving not from its overthrow of history but from its capitulation [surrender] to it.

Interestingly, the character in the novel who most fully embodies that capitulation to history is Madame Defarge, the figure in the story who is also most likely to be misunderstood. As a worker, and particularly as a woman, Thérèsa Defarge would seem to have more to gain than anyone else from a successful assault on patrilineal culture and the historical record that supports it. . . . But in fact there is no more ferociously dedicated historian in *A Tale of Two Cities* than Madame Defarge. True, the medium of the historical record she compiles is the traditionally female one of knitting, but in no sense does that activity perform the domestic function of, say, Lucie Manette's sewing. For though Madame Defarge writes her history with matriarchal needles and yarn, she is as obsessed with genealogy as the most unreconstructed patriarchal aristocrat, wholly committed, like that aristocrat, to judging her fellow human beings not by their abilities or by their actions (in the anti-historical spirit of, for instance, the First Reform Bill) but entirely by their birth. It is on this principle that she persists in hunting down the innocent Charles Darnay and his even more innocent wife and child. But her obsession with the authority of the historical record is carried to even greater lengths. Called upon to select between the living testimony of Doctor Manette and the obsolete account of his earlier, vengeful autobiography, she chooses—and forces the whole of the Revolution to choose with her—the past over the present, the historical over the personal, the moribund written word over the living man. Not by chance is her second-in-command called "The Vengeance," a fact that for Dickens deeply compromises the revolutionary ideal since desire for revenge constitutes the ultimate surrender to history. . . .

It is in the celebrated final chapter of *A Tale of Two Cities* that Dickens finally advances, as he had hoped he would, beyond . . . historical speculations . . . literary colleagues to point a way out of this impasse; although the scene in the Place de Guillotine that chapter describes seems, at first, merely to recapitulate the old dilemma. In the background are all the familiar emblems of a mechanical and enervating historical science. The tumbrils move heavily toward the square, bearing their burdens of old histories, past injustices, like the cartloads of books Carlyle mockingly sent to Dickens. . . . And it is history as a machine of death that is symbolized by the brisk, mindless working of the guillotine.

In the foreground, set against this vast, impersonal public display, is the preternaturally private relationship of Sydney Carton and the young seamstress (who sews, we may presume, rather than knits). Entirely silent about his own fate out of concern for the girl's, Carton advises her to see and think of nothing around her, to ignore, as it were, past and future and live only in the immediate present, advice in which we may recognize a curiously transfigured version of the irresponsible behavior that had earlier blighted his own career. But here that antihistorical behavior leads to intimacy not isolation, and Carton's silence is the silence not of one who withdraws himself from the world but rather of one who withholds himself for the sake of another, is mute in order to permit another to speak, a familiar Dickensian resolution. Again, there is a foreshadowing of this resolution in Carton's earlier activities as a brief writer whose name never appears on his work. That namelessness also returns in a new form at the end of the story. For Carton, choosing to die under the name of another, decisively repudiates the absurd mechanics of genealogical connection. While the seamstress, who is herself nameless and who, we learn, cannot write, demonstrates the insignificance of formal history in the face of an even momentary living bond.

As much of an enemy as Dickens was of the mechanical and formal, however, it was never any part of his desire to repudiate genealogy and history in themselves any more than he wished to promote revolutionary anarchy. Indeed, as a writer he had the greatest possible stake in preserving the authority of texts, the immediacy and vitality of the written record, and in *A Tale of Two Cities* in particular he undertook to span what to others seemed the unbridgeable gulf between history and life, to make these two cities one. The whole book is artfully structured to achieve this goal, though Dickens' point only becomes fully clear on the last page where Sydney Carton, about to mount the scaffold, pauses to prophesy about events that are to follow his death.... "I see," the prophetic speaker intones, alluding here to Charles and Lucie,

> that I hold a sanctuary in their hearts, and in the hearts of descendents, generations hence ... I see that child who lay upon her bosom and bore my name, a man winning his way up that path of life which once was mine. I see him winning it so well that my name is made illustrious there by the light

of his. . . . I see him . . . bringing a boy of my name . . . to this place . . . *and I hear him tell the child my story*, with a tender and faltering voice. [italics mine]

What is so striking about this passage is how full of genealogy and history it is. In his last moments, Carton returns obsessively to thoughts of "descendents," of "generations," of those who will one day bear his name; in particular, he is preoccupied with the image of a child yet unborn who, growing into a man, will become the historian of his present sacrifice. These, however, it is clear, are genealogy and history with a difference, not baleful voices from the past with dread authority to impose upon and enervate the present, but rather in Dickens' powerful proleptic [showing something to exist before its proper historical time] vision, a vitalizing genealogy and history of the future.

The whole of *A Tale of Two Cities* shares in this prolepsis. Whatever present moment we may have arrived at in the story, for instance, the book's rich texture of foreshadowings operates to urge us toward moments still to come. Footsteps advancing on the future haunt the novel, paradoxically "echoing" sounds that have not yet been made; and these foreshadowings, taken together, themselves constitute a meta-foreshadowing of the Carton prophecy. Even death is forced out of the service of the past, for, described from the start as a "farmer" with furrow-plowing tumbrils, as a sower, death can, despite its worst intentions, only prepare the ground for new life. And, of course, Dickens gains considerable support for the validity of his foresight from the fact that the speculative future about which he has his hero prophesy is already the confirmed past and present of his readers.

The Carton/Dickens ideal of a history of the future that will rescue the nineteenth century from the history of the past is more than just figurative, however. The chief adverse power of the past is, we have seen, its ability to dash the hopes of the present and blight the future. Just to be able to *imagine* a vital future, then (the novel suggests), is already in a very practical way to have defeated the worst that the past can do. . . . [*A Tale of Two Cities* is] a book that, in the face of profound nineteenth-century disillusionment about the uses of the past, argues for a kind of history that is not a nightmare. In Dickens' celebratory conclusion to *A Tale of Two Cities*, Sydney Carton awakes both out of the history of his dead past and into the history of a living future.

A Tale of Two Cities as Great Drama

Richard J. Dunn

According to Richard J. Dunn, a literary scholar and member of the editorial board of the prestigious journal *Dickens Studies Annual*, both Charles Dickens and his friend Thomas Carlyle treated the French Revolution as a huge theatrical event, a dramatic play in "a theater for history." In his influential work *The French Revolution*, notes Dunn, Carlyle refers to the "theatricality of a people," and a "scenic exhibition" more natural to the French than to the English; and in *A Tale of Two Cities*, Dickens often employs phrases such as "until the play is played out." According to Dunn, both books openly dramatize history, and should be viewed as melodramas (which have a reputation for being more show than substance). However, he adds, first-rate melodramas like these do readily lend themselves to the exploration of important ideas and values.

The first historians of the French Revolution often spoke of it as a play . . . [and scholarship has shown that] participants in the revolution were aware that their world had become a theater. That Carlyle's and Dickens' works often regard revolutionary figures as actors, describe crowds of people as engaged audiences, and treat many historical events as performances is evident to any reader of *The French Revolution* and *A Tale of Two Cities*. As Michael Goldberg [author of *Carlyle and Dickens*] has said, the dramatic mode of these books is a natural stylistic concomitant of the writers' view of the revolution as a process working itself out in moral terms. For Carlyle and Dickens the French Revolution was indeed a great drama, and each attempted to write about it dramatically. I am aware that subject matter was not the sole

Excerpted from "A Tale for Two Dramatists" by Richard J. Dunn, *Dickens Studies Annual*, vol. 12 (1983), pp. 117-23. Reprinted by permission of AMS Press, New York, N.Y.

determinant of style for either author, but in this paper I want briefly to consider how each regarded the revolution as a great drama yet also took into account the grave dangers of mere theatrical performance in the revolution.

Artificial Versus Mechanical Performance

There is, as Carlyle especially recognized, an essential duplicity in the words "drama," "theatrical," "actor." Throughout his works he, on the one hand, celebrates history as cosmic drama and insists upon action and articulation as primary modes of heroism. On the other hand, he scorns the merely histrionic and artificial, the masquerading and mimicry of a people unable to enact their true roles. In his history of the French Revolution Carlyle stresses the distinction between significant and insignificant drama, meaningful and ineffectual action. He describes the uprising as a great dramatic event, "a great Phenomenon . . . a *transcendental* one, overstepping all rules and experience; the crowning Phenomenon of our Modern Time." Much was only noise and chaos, and, as Carlyle remarks, the Bastille seemed to fall by miraculous sound. Noisy phases of fever-frenzy burst forth in Carlyle's account, but he argues that the frenzy burns itself out so a new order may arise. Behind this claim is Carlyle's faith in the irrevocable word, the action completed. "What," he asks, "is this Infinite of Things itself, which men name Universe, but an Action, a sum-total of Actions and Activities?" Such might serve as the definition of a superb play, for that also is a sum of actions, unified by some sort of meaning. In Carlyle's great life drama, heroic speech and action are both enactments of transcendental faith. To Carlyle's thinking, the quality of the play is the thing to be watched. Imposture, masquerading as the real thing, is the great evil, and the penultimate paragraph of Carlyle's history celebrates a fiery purging of Imposture—"one red sea of Fire, wild-billowing, enwraps the World." So describing the result of the revolution, Carlyle maintains his moral that "all grows and seeks and endures its destinies."

So much for the grand outcome. Along the way Carlyle often attempts to distinguish true from false, genuine human drama from artificial and mechanical performance, meaning from nonmeaning. He is most self-conscious of this effort about half way through his history, in the chapter titled "Symbolic." He begins the chapter pointing out the naturalness of all symbolic representation: life, says Carlyle, is the act and word striving to make visible a "Celestial invisible Force." How best to do it? "With sincerity if possible; failing that, with theatricality, which . . . also may have its meaning."

For an author ever so vigilant against sham and so impatient with mere performance—those wearers of costumes and dancers on ropes—Carlyle here seems surprisingly tolerant in his recognition that often we have "Imagination herself flagging under the reality; and all noblest Ceremony as yet not grown ceremonial but solemn, significant to the outmost fringe." His reasoning seems to be that intent may be sincere even when the performance or ceremony is questionable. "No Nation," he continues, "will throw by its work, and deliberately go out to make a scene without meaning something thereby." Moreover, "no scenic individual, with knavish hypocritical views, will take the trouble to *soliloquize* a scene." He grants that "scenic exhibition" is more natural to French than to English people, and he postulates that the "theatricality of a People goes in a compound ratio: ratio indeed of their trustfulness, sociability, fervency; but then also of their excitability, of their porosity, . . . or say, of their explosiveness, hot-flashing." Viewed in this way, much human theatricality is pardonable for Carlyle, because he regards it as "the passionate utterance of a tongue with which sincerity stammers; of a head with which insincerity babbles,—having gone distracted.". . .

To Carlyle, then, the grand phenomenon of the French Revolution was a spectacular dramatic event in human history. Its violence may point up the hazard of spontaneity, but its lesson is clear: "the beginning of man's doom is, that vision be withdrawn from him; that he sees not the reality, but a false spectrum of the reality." The dramatic struggle his book presents is one of anarchy (revolutionists acting without clear vision) versus an intolerable posturing authority. At this level the opposition is absolute, and the play as clear-cut as melodrama. But in the world view of Carlyle there is more complication through a sense of tragic division between mere human theatricality and the "everliving Heart of Nature." Strain between artifice and truth remains evident in Carlyle's concluding prophetic statement:

> For whatsoever once sacred things become hollow jargons, yet while the Voice of Man speaks with Man, hast thou not there the living fountain out of which all sacrednesses

sprang, and yet will spring? Man, by the nature of him, is definable as "an incarnated Word." Ill stands it with me if I have spoken falsely: thine also it was to hear truly Farewell.

The curtain is down but the curtain speech reverberates with the philosophy behind Carlyle's own performance as he concludes self-consciously (almost like an actor stepping to the front at the end of a play) and sincerely to underscore the value of the transcending word.

THE SUM OF EVENTS GREATER THAN ANY CHARACTER

In *A Tale of Two Cities* the sense of performance, especially in the dramatic climax, is often more overt than any philosophy behind it. Dickens came to the novel fresh from amateur theatricals; the idea for the rebirth theme comes from the stage as well as from urgencies in his private life.... Dickens in *A Tale of Two Cities* had an actor's sense of participating in a chosen role....

Rather than to point ... to many of the dramatic devices and consider their effectiveness, I want to indicate how *A Tale of Two Cities* incorporates Carlyle's sense of the greater drama, the revolution as a "great Phenomenon." Consider, first, that letter in which Dickens discusses the kind of book he is writing. He speaks of

> a *picturesque* story, rising in every chapter with characters true to nature, but whom the story itself should express, more than they should express themselves, by dialogue. I mean, in other words, that I fancied a story of incident might be written, in place of the odious stuff that is written under that pretense.

It is questionable whether Dickens was more dramatic here than in some other novels, but he certainly was more austere in style. The key issue is his commitment to characters "true to nature." In this he directly follows Carlyle, for his insistence upon truth to nature reiterates Carlyle's stress upon sincerity. In having story dominate character, Dickens also follows Carlyle by writing history with a controlling thesis about the tide of events cumulatively enforcing a lesson. The sum of events, greater than any of those innumerable biographies Carlyle elsewhere defined as history, is more important than the story of any character caught up in those events, even than the romantically tragic story of Sydney Carton.

For Dickens, as for Carlyle, there is meaning and connectedness in the scheme of things. Proof of that in *A Tale of Two Cities* depends mainly upon the Carton-Darnay-Manette domestic story where coincidence figures so prominently. Cringe though many readers do because of the sentimental and melodramatic aspects of this story, we should keep in mind Dickens' larger purpose. In the same letter describing his determination to write picturesquely with character subordinate to event, he indicated distaste for "odious stuff . . . written under the pretense" of being significant. Taken with the praise his preface gives to Carlyle's history, this statement must be taken as a sign of Dickens' seriousness, and his intention to set his work apart from popular theater concurs with Carlyle's expressed scorn for mere theatricality.

That Dickens was serious indeed is evident by the opening of his third chapter where he ponders "the wonderful fact . . . that every human creature is constituted to be that profound secret and mystery to every other." The death of a loved one, especially, reminds him of "the secret that was always in that individuality." This is one of Dickens' most overt Carlylean statements, not only because it employs Carlyle's rhetorical tactic of stressing the wonder of facts but particularly because it respects an essential incommunicability of "innermost personality." As in earlier novels which acknowledged the power of the uncanny, Dickens here in his third chapter speaks of darkly clustered houses, each enclosing its own secret and containing an awfulness contrasting the triviality of much public life. *A Tale of Two Cities* pictures many public spectacles—the spilling of the wine, the collapse of the Bastille, the sharpening of the knives, the dancing in the streets, and the scenes in court—but we need to remember that this book also remains sensitive to a buried life, to inarticulate and mysterious depths. Carlyle, discussing natural and symbolic expression, had spoken of the celestial force invisible within, and early in *A Tale of Two Cities* Dickens acknowledges a similar resource.

Granted, much of the revolution, as traced in the novel, has no respect for secrets. The ciphers in the woman's knitting become an executioner's list of victims; more ironically, Dr. Manette's secret manuscript turns into the death sentence for his son-in-law. The chief keeper of secrets, Sydney, goes to his death with what some in the crowd might recognize as a sublime and prophetic face, but his famous last words, conveyed to us by a fellow-victim, are appropriately after the fact of his heroic action. The words but not the action remain problematic. Their effect upon both immediate and future audiences contrasts the definitive quality of Sydney's sacrifice. The final scene, then, is most literally a translation of word into deed, act into meaning, and it epitomizes behavior Carlyle hailed as heroic.

A THEATER FOR HISTORY

Study of the various courtroom scenes and of a number of other performances in *A Tale of Two Cities* would indicate that Dickens was very aware of the history presenting itself as drama and of people coming across as poor players. Recall, for example, how the road-mender seeking sanctuary with the Defarges fears Thérèse as he foresees her continuing her knitting "until the play is played out."

Without Dickens' underlying and explicitly Carlylean sense of a substantial inarticulate life, the novel would at best be pathetic in its statement about the French Revolution. There is no question that many of the narrative devices are melodramatic and sentimental in the most pejorative senses of those terms, but we should take the melodramatic structure seriously. Melodrama, as a technique, is usually oversimple and often mechanical. So, too often, is the idea of revolution. . . . Carlyle had spoken of revolution as a violent kind of growth toward a destiny, and so too does Dickens finish with a sense of the revolution's grand accomplishment. His final chapter starts with the familiar passage about the tumbrils rumbling on through the Paris streets and on through history. He warns of a horror that may return if humanity is ever again so crushed out of shape, and Dickens continues with an echo of the final passage of Carlyle's book, once more treating the French Revolution as the overthrow of imposture:

> Six tumbrils roll along the streets. Change these back again to what they were, thou powerful enchanter, Time, and they shall be seen to be the carriages of absolute monarchs, the equipages of feudal nobles, the toilettes of flaring Jezebels, the churches that are not my father's house but dens of thieves, the huts of millions of starving peasants! No; the great magician who majestically works out the appointed order of the Creator, never reverses his transformations. . . . Changeless and hopeless, the tumbrils roll along.

"Time" to Dickens' thinking, and indeed in many an earlier Dickens fairy tale, is certainly a "powerful enchanter," but here Dickens sounds a more serious Carlylean note of respect for time as a scope of dramatic action, a theater for history. Note especially his metaphors of performance when he speaks of the royal carriages, equipages, toilettes. With the elaborate props, the former rulers of France seemed always to present themselves as performers. As surely as the conclusion of *The French Revolution* describes the fiery consumption of thrones, mitres, pretentious "Wheel-vehicles," so too does Dickens here envision the transformation of sham.

But rather than append an epilogue as had Carlyle when using the "Voice of a Man" speaking with "Man" to defy hollow jargons, Dickens adds the "sublime" example of Carton's death. I have already nominated Carton as an exemplary Carlylean hero, one who achieves the satisfaction of sincere action. A slight emendation [alteration] of his famous last thoughts may therefore be in order to underscore my point: "It is a far, far better thing I do than anything I have ever said."

I have looked at a few important connections between *The French Revolution* and *A Tale of Two Cities* to suggest the authors shared not only assumptions about the historical event's instructive importance but also about it as an occasion for enacting what Carlyle valued as human "trustfulness, sociability, fervency" on a stage remarkable for more explosive and terrifying theatricality. A separate study might focus more on the performances of Carlyle and Dickens themselves, for both were chief actors as narrators. I have dwelt more on what they seemed to be up to than on the quality of what they achieved. Opponents of mere theatricality in the conduct of private and public life, both Carlyle and Dickens nonetheless employed a number of theatrical devices as they responded to the profound drama of the French Revolution. Flaws in their productions may be evident, and evidently may be accounted for in a number of ways. But Carlyle and Dickens deserve applause as melodramatists. Both presented their subjects with the polemic intention common to melodrama; both centered their attention in those realms of social and public action that are the subject locales of melodrama.... We certainly too often dismiss melodrama as a matter of shock effects, but... melodrama also quite legitimately traffics in ideas and makes use of fundamental concepts and values. As two dramatists, Carlyle and Dickens were melodramatists, pointing out extremes but remembering also to value humanity and to be wary of posturing performance.

Dickens's *Tale* Attempts to Break History's Chain of Violence

J.M. Rignall

Some historians and philosophers interpret history as an unbroken chain of violent events—as scholar Walter Benjamin has put it, a single catastrophe, piling wreckage on wreckage. In the following essay, J.M. Rignall of the University of Warwick refers to this dangerous chain as the "catastrophic continuum of history," a cycle of violence that, Rignall contends, Dickens sought to break in writing *A Tale of Two Cities*. The author's main device to that end was Sydney Carton's climactic sacrifice, which supposedly held out hope for a better world beyond the current historical cycle. According to Rignall, however, Dickens failed to break the cycle, partly because Carton, despite his heroic act, ends up as just another "victim of socio-historical circumstances," and also because Dickens exposed a violent side of himself in his personal life while writing the novel.

It is not surprising that the most remembered scene in *A Tale of Two Cities* is the last, for this novel is dominated, even haunted, by its ending. From the opening chapter in which the "creatures of this chronicle" are set in motion "along the roads that lay before them," while the Woodman Fate and the Farmer Death go silently about their ominous work, those roads lead with sinister inevitability to the revolutionary scaffold. To an unusual extent, especially given the expansive and centrifugal nature of Dickens's imagination, this is an end-determined narrative whose individual elements are ordered by an ending which is both their goal and, in a sense, their source. In a historical novel like this there is a transparent relationship between narrative form

Excerpted from "Dickens and the Catastrophic Continuum of History in *A Tale of Two Cities*" by J.M. Rignall, *ELH*, vol. 51, no. 3 (Fall 1984), pp. 575-86. Copyright ©1984 by and reprinted with permission from The Johns Hopkins University Press.

and historical vision, and the formal features of *A Tale*—its emphatic linearity, continuity, and negative teleology [purposeful development toward a finale]—define a distinctive vision of history. . . . It is not the particular historical event that ultimately concerns Dickens here, but rather a wider view of history and the historical process. That process is a peculiarly grim one. As oppression is shown to breed oppression, violence to beget violence, evil to provoke evil, a pattern emerges that is too deterministic to owe much to Carlyle and profoundly at odds with the conventional complacencies of Whig history. Instead of progress there is something more like the catastrophic continuum that is [scholar] Walter Benjamin's description of the historical process: the single catastrophe, piling wreckage upon wreckage. And when, in the sentimental postscript of Carton's prophecy, Dickens finally attempts to envisage a liberation from this catastrophic process, he can only do so, like Benjamin, in eschatological terms [those dealing with the end of the world and final destiny]. For Benjamin it was the messianic intervention of a proletarian revolution that would bring time to a standstill and blast open the continuum of history; for Dickens it is the Christ-like intervention of a self-sacrificing individual that is the vehicle for a vision of a better world which seems to lie beyond time and history. . . . The coexistence of these two elements in *A Tale* is, I wish to argue, important for an understanding of the novel, lending it a peculiarly haunted and contradictory quality as Dickens gives expression to a vision of history which both compels and repels him at the same time.

A CHAIN OF VIOLENT EVENTS

In Carton's final vision of a world seemingly beyond time, the paradigm of the apocalypse mediates between what is known of history and what may be hoped for it. That hope is not to be dismissed as mere sentimentality, whatever the manner of its expression. However inadequately realized Carton's prophecy may be in imaginative terms, it is significant as a moment of resistance to the grimly terminal linearity and historical determinism of the preceding narrative. That resistance is not confined to the last page of the novel, for, as I shall show, it manifests itself in other places and in other ways, creating a faint but discernible counter-current to the main thrust of the narrative. This is not to say that

Dickens presents a thorough-going deconstruction of his own narrative procedures and version of history in *A Tale*, for the process at work here is more ambiguous and tentative than that. There is a struggle with sombre fears that gives rise to contradictions which cannot be reduced to the internal self-contradictions of language. What the novel presents is, rather, the spectacle of an imagination both seized by a compelling vision of history as a chain of violence, a catastrophic continuum, and impelled to resist that vision in the very act of articulation, so that the narrative seems at the same time to seek and to shun the violent finality of its ending in the Terror. The nightmare vision is too grim to accept without protest, and too powerful to be dispelled by simple hopefulness, and the work bears the signs of this unresolved and unresolvable contradiction.

In his preface Dickens maintains that the idea of the novel had "complete possession" of him, and the state of imaginative obsession in which *A Tale of Two Cities* was written can be sensed in two rather different aspects of the work: in the way that it presses on relentlessly toward its violent ending, and in the way that particular scenes take on a visionary intensity, seemingly charged with obscure and powerful emotions that are neither fully controlled nor comprehended. . . .

Although Dickens primarily uses the death of Carton and the ending of the novel to complete a pattern of meaning rather than to effect a premature closure, there are occasions in the novel when the desire for such a closure surfaces in the text as if in reaction to the chain of violent events that leads relentlessly to the guillotine. The first-person plural dramatization of the Darnays' flight from Paris provides, for instance, a kind of alternative premature ending for those privileged characters who are allowed to escape the logic of the historical process. . . . It is a flight which necessarily carries the characters beyond the boundaries of the novel, which is headed to only one conclusion, and they never again appear directly in it. Pursued not by the Revolution but, as it turns out, only by a reflection of their own fears, they may be said to be escaping from history: "the wind is rushing after us, and the clouds are flying after us, and the moon is plunging after us, and the whole wild night is in pursuit of us; but, so far we are pursued by nothing else." In fleeing the ending of the novel they have fled beyond the process of history.

A SPECTACLE OF BESTIAL VIOLENCE

There is a less direct and more complex suggestion of flight from the grim logic of the historical process in the scene of the mob around the grindstone, observed by Mr. Lorry and Dr. Manette. What they witness is an appalling spectacle of bestial violence and moral degradation as Dickens lets his wildest and deepest fears rise to the surface. The chain reaction of violent oppression and violent rebellion has passed beyond human control, and in this mass frenzy all distinctions of individuality and even sex are submerged:

> The eye could not detect one creature in the group free from the smear of blood. Shouldering one another to get next at the sharpening-stone, were men stripped to the waist, with the stain all over their limbs and bodies; men in all sorts of rags, with the stain upon those rags; men devilishly set off with spoils of women's lace and silk and ribbon, with the stain dyeing those trifles through and through. . . .

> And as the frantic wielders of these weapons snatched them from the stream of sparks and tore away into the streets, the same red hue was red in their frenzied eyes;—eyes which any unbrutalised beholder would have given twenty years of life, to petrify with a well-directed gun.

> All this was seen in a moment, as the vision of a drowning man, or of any human creature at any very great pass, could see a world if it were there. They drew back from the window, and the Doctor looked for explanation in his friend's ashy face.

Clearly signalled as the vision of a drowning man, the scene is the product of an imagination *in extremis.* It is a bourgeois nightmare of anarchy unleashed by the rebellion of the oppressed. Even if it is the logical culmination of the violent oppression that has preceded it, the violence is, when it eventuates, too great to bear. . . . The curious insistence on the eyes of the frenzied crowd emphasizes that vision is the vital element, and the urge to "petrify" those eyes can be read as the expression of a desire to put an end to that vision. The action is transposed from subject to object: it is not their eyes that Dickens the narrator wishes to close, but his own. For a moment he seeks to retreat from his own vision of the historical process.

There is, then, a form of resistance here to the catastrophic continuum of history, but at the same time Dickens reveals something about the emotional dynamics of that historical process in a way that is more penetrating than the melodramatic simplifications of Madame Defarge and her desire for vengeance. The violent . . . answering of violence with violence implicates the writer himself in the very process he is presenting. This is characteristic of the open and unguarded nature of his procedure in *A Tale*: violent fears and violent reactions are given direct, unmediated expression, so that unwitting parallels emerge between the reflexes of the author/narrator and those of the fictional characters. . . . Dickens thus does more than simply project a deterministic vision of history; he shows how that determinism is rooted in commonplace and familiar emotions, how the potential for violence is not confined to a savage past and an alien setting, but lies very close to home. The effect is to detach history from the safety of the past and to suggest that its violent continuum may not have expired with the Revolution.

Beating His Own Characters

The persistence of that violence is amply demonstrated by Dickens's own susceptibility to the kinds of powerful emotions that are at work in the novel. As a caricature of the conquering bourgeois, the figure of Stryver belongs as much in the nineteenth century as the eighteenth, and Dickens himself could display distinctly Stryverish leanings in his response to contemporary events. In the same letter to [his friend John] Forster in which he outlines his intentions in *A Tale of Two Cities* and which he must have written about the same time as the grindstone passage, there is a revealing outburst of verbal violence. The letter begins with a discussion of the case of the surgeon Thomas Smethurst, found guilty of poisoning his bigamous "wife." The trial judge, Sir Jonathan Frederick Pollock, strongly supported the verdict in the face of public unease and of moves to persuade the Home Secretary to quash or commute the sentence. Dickens gives his fervent support to Pollock, and in doing so presents another example of an outraged, violent reaction to an act of violence:

> I followed the case with so much interest, and have followed the miserable knaves and asses who have perverted it since, with so much indignation, that I have often had more than half a mind to write and thank the upright judge who tried him. I declare to God that I believe such a service one of the greatest that a man of intellect and courage can render to society. Of course I saw the beast of a prisoner (with my mind's

eye) delivering his cut-and-dried speech, and read in every word of it that no one but the murderer could have delivered or conceived it. Of course I have been driving the girls out of their wits here, by incessantly proclaiming that there needed no medical evidence either way, and that the case was plain without it. Lastly, of course (though a merciful man—because a merciful man I mean), I would hang any Home Secretary (Whig, Tory, Radical, or otherwise) who should step in between that black scoundrel and the gallows.

... What is more interesting, however, is that the violence spills over into his account [from the same letter to Forster] of his intentions in writing *A Tale*:

But I set myself the little task of making a *picturesque* story, rising in every chapter with characters true to nature, but whom the story itself should express, more than they should express themselves, by dialogue. I mean, in other words, that I have fancied a story of incident might be written, in place of the bestiality that *is* written under that pretence, pounding the characters out in its own mortar, and beating their own interests out of them. If you could have read the story all at once, I hope you wouldn't have stopped half way.

As violent an exception is taken to conventional forms of storytelling as is taken to an alleged murderer, and when Dickens writes of "pounding" and "beating" his characters it seems that violence is not only central to his vision of history in this novel but is also inherent in his means of expressing that vision. This formal violence, which could be interpreted in one sense as the forcible subordination of character to the story of incident, is as revealingly related to the creation of a narrative and historical continuum as is the earlier emotional violence. The expressed intention is to prevent the reader from stopping halfway, to maintain a compelling momentum in the narrative, and this momentum also serves the vision of historical determinism by subjecting individuals to a sequence of violent events that is beyond their power to control.

What exactly Dickens means by beating his characters' own interest out of them is open to question. ... The only character who has any real interest to be beaten out of him, Carton, is not the object of any direct allegorizing. Indeed, in his case meaning is deliberately withheld rather than allegorically asserted, and no cogent reasons are offered for his alienation. This mystification has the effect of directing the search for significance away from the personal life towards the general condition of existence. ... Carton comes to stand, too, as the victim of the catastrophic continuum of history, a role which he then, at the end, consciously assumes.

AN ACT BOTH PERVERSE AND NOBLE

To define Carton in these terms is to spell out bluntly what is only intimated indirectly, for it is Dickens's refusal to define and explain precisely that gives Carton a greater degree of density and interest than the other characters. . . . If, as Benjamin argues, the meaning of the life of a character in a novel is revealed in his death, then Carton could be said to constitute himself as a character by choosing to die by the guillotine. He gives himself a goal and a purpose, and in so doing gives shape and meaning to his life. What has been aimless and indefinite becomes purposive and defined, and continuity is established between beginning and end, between promising youth and exemplary death. He achieves character in both a formal and a moral sense. . . .

Carton's transformation is clearly intended to be read as the redemption of a wasted life, but such a reading has to ignore the qualifying ambiguities that are involved in it. As he decides on his course of action, resolution is strangely mixed with fatalism:

> "There is nothing more to do," said he, glancing upward at the moon, "until tomorrow. I can't sleep."

> It was not a reckless manner, the manner in which he said these words aloud under the fast-sailing clouds, nor was it more expressive of negligence than defiance. It was the settled manner of a tired man, who had wandered and struggled and got lost, but who at length struck into his road and saw its end.

The term "end" carries a double meaning: in one sense it has to be read as "goal," stressing Carton's new-found sense of purpose and smuggling into the novel on the level of the individual life the positive teleology that is so markedly absent on the level of history. But the stronger meaning here is that of "conclusion," and a conclusion that is approached with a sense of release rather than a sense of achievement. The "tired man" is simply seeking repose, and in his desire for an end he makes explicit that resistance to the narrative and historical continuum which has been intimated elsewhere in the novel and now surfaces as the deepest yearning of a particular character.

He wishes to escape but, significantly, the mode of escape he chooses merely confirms his status as a victim of socio-historical circumstances. The act of self-sacrifice—an idea which haunts Dickens's imagination in this novel as powerfully and melodramatically as images of revolutionary violence—cannot be seen as simply the ultimate expression of altruism, since it is obscurely rooted in the same values that have significantly contributed to Carton's estrangement in the first place. The puritan ethic of disciplined personal endeavor demands renunciation such as Carton has been neurotically making all along, and its final act is the renunciation of life itself. Thus the very step which makes sense of his life is as perverse as it is noble, as much a capitulation to the uncontrollable forces that have governed his life as a transcendence of them. To seek to escape sacrifice by sacrificing oneself is the expression of a truly desperate desire for an ending. . . .

Weariness, both of character and of creative imagination, is the keynote of this ending, and it betrays the intellectual and imaginative impasse in which Dickens finds himself. Since he sees revolution as just another link in the chain of violence and oppression, and presents the efforts of individuals, like Darnay's journey to Paris, as powerless to influence the course of historical events, he can conceive no possibility, to use Benjamin's phrase, of blasting open the continuum of history by social and political action. Unlike Benjamin, Dickens can advance no alternative vision of time and history. . . . Even the moments of discontinuity discussed earlier only challenge the narrative and historical continuum by revealing a desire to evade it. Carton's prophecy is simply a final evasive move, and one that gives itself away by its weary insistence on death and its eschatological suggestion of the end of time. Only by turning away from the course of human history can Dickens find a refuge for hope, and to express hope in such terms is tantamount to a confession of despair. In this novel of imprisonments and burials alive the writer himself remains imprisoned in a rigorously linear, end-determined narrative and the grimly determinist vision of history which it articulates. The resistance he offers is that of a mind vainly struggling to escape and thereby confirming the power of that which holds it captive. This vision of history as a catastrophic continuum is only made more powerful by the clear indications in the text that Dickens is expressing what is deeply repugnant to, yet stronger than, all that he can hope and wish for.

CHRONOLOGY

1812
Charles Dickens is born in Landport, England; the War of 1812 erupts between Great Britain and the United States; French dictator Napoléon Bonaparte invades Russia.

1814
Dickens's mother, Elizabeth, begins teaching him to read; Great Britain and the United States sign the Treaty of Ghent, ending the War of 1812.

1821
Dickens begins attending school.

1824
After his father, John, is sent to debtors' prison, Dickens goes to work at Warren's Blacking factory; after three months, upon his father's release from prison, he begins attending Wellington House Academy in London.

1831
Dickens becomes a reporter for the *Mirror of Parliament.*

1834
Dickens acquires the position of staff writer on the *Morning Chronicle*; meets his future wife, Catherine Hogarth.

1836
Dickens publishes *Sketches by Boz*; marries Catherine Hogarth; meets John Forster, who will later become his first important biographer.

1837
Dickens's *Oliver Twist* first appears in installments in *Bentley's Miscellany*; his first child is born; at age eighteen, Victoria, granddaughter of King George III, becomes queen of Great Britain, initiating the Victorian era, the longest reign (1837–1901) of any British monarch in history.

1842
Dickens and his wife tour the United States; he publishes *American Notes* and begins work on *Martin Chuzzlewit.*

1845

Dickens writes *The Cricket on the Hearth*; his fourth son is born; a blight destroys Ireland's potato crop, initiating a terrible famine.

1846

Dickens begins writing *Dombey and Son*; the British Parliament repeals the Corn Laws, which kept food prices artificially high and thereby worsened the Irish potato famine, a move that begins a period of increasing free trade and overall prosperity for the British.

1849

Dickens begins writing *David Copperfield*; his sixth son is born.

1852

Bleak House appears in monthly installments; Dickens's seventh son is born; American writer Harriet Beecher Stowe publishes *Uncle Tom's Cabin*, a graphic description of American slavery, which contributes to the spread of the abolitionist movement in the United States.

1859

Dickens establishes a new weekly magazine, *All the Year Round*, in which *A Tale of Two Cities* appears in installments from April 20 to November 26; the novel is published in book form in December.

1860

Dickens launches installments of *Great Expectations*.

1865

Dickens suffers a stroke and is also involved in a train accident; his *Our Mutual Friend* appears in book form.

1867

Dickens travels again to the United States, where he gives readings of his works in Boston and New York; pushed by the increasingly powerful legislator Benjamin Disraeli, the British Parliament passes the Second Reform Bill, extending the vote to many portions of the labor force and doubling the electorate.

1870

Dickens dies in Gad's Hill Place near London at age fifty-eight; he is buried in the prestigious Poet's Corner in Westminster Abbey.

FOR FURTHER RESEARCH

ABOUT DICKENS'S LIFE AND TIMES

Peter Ackroyd, *Dickens*. New York: HarperCollins, 1990.

M.A. Crowther, *The Workhouse System 1834–1929: The History of an English Social Institution*. Athens: University of Georgia Press, 1981.

Clive Emsley, *Crime and Society in England, 1750–1900*. London: Longman, 1987.

K.J. Fielding, ed., *The Speeches of Charles Dickens, A Complete Edition*. Atlantic Highlands, NJ: Harvester Wheatsheaf, 1988.

John Forster, *The Life of Charles Dickens*. 1874. Reprinted, London: Dent, 1966, A.J. Hoppé, ed.

Robert Giddings, ed., *The Changing World of Charles Dickens*. London: Vision Press, 1983.

Fred Kaplan, *Dickens: A Biography*. New York: William Morrow 1988.

Kenneth O. Morgan, ed., *The Oxford Illustrated History of Britain*. New York: Oxford University Press, 1986.

David Morse, *High Victorian Culture*. New York: New York University Press, 1993.

Paul Schlicke, *Dickens and Popular Entertainment*. London: Allen and Unwin, 1985.

F.M.L. Thompson, *The Rise of Respectable Society: A Social History of Victorian Britain 1830–1900*. Cambridge, MA: Harvard University Press, 1988.

Angus Wilson, *The World of Charles Dickens*. New York: Viking Press, 1970.

ABOUT DICKENS'S WRITING STYLE AND WORKS

William F. Axton, *Circle of Fire: Dickens' Vision and Style and the Popular Victorian Theater*. Lexington: University of Kentucky Press, 1956.

Harold Bloom, ed., *Charles Dickens: Modern Critical Views.* New York: Chelsea House, 1987.

Philip Collins, ed., *Dickens: The Critical Heritage.* London: Routledge and Kegan Paul, 1971.

H.M. Daleski, *Dickens and the Art of Analogy.* New York: Schocken Books, 1970.

A.E. Dyson, *The Inimitable Dickens: A Reading of the Novels.* London: Macmillan, 1970.

George R. Gissing, *Critical Studies of the Works of Charles Dickens.* New York: Greenberg Press, 1924.

Audrey Jaffe, *Vanishing Points: Dickens, Narrative, and the Subject of Omniscience.* Berkeley: University of California Press, 1991.

John Kucich, *Excess and Restraint in the Novels of Charles Dickens.* Athens: University of Georgia Press, 1981.

Frank Lawrence, *Charles Dickens and the Romantic Self.* Lincoln: University of Nebraska Press, 1984.

Martin Price, ed., *Dickens: A Collection of Critical Essays.* Englewood Cliffs, NJ: Prentice Hall, 1967.

John R. Reed, *Dickens and Thackeray: Punishment and Forgiveness.* Athens: Ohio University Press, 1995.

Garrett Stewart, *Death Sentences: Styles of Dying in British Fiction.* Cambridge, MA: Harvard University Press, 1984.

Deborah Thomas, *Dickens and the Short Story.* Philadelphia: University of Pennsylvania Press, 1982.

Geoffrey Thurley, *The Dickens Myth: Its Genesis and Structure.* New York: St. Martin's Press, 1976.

Jane Vogel, *Allegory in Dickens.* University: University of Alabama Press, 1977.

Dennis Walder, *Dickens and Religion.* London: George Allen and Unwin, 1981.

ABOUT *A TALE OF TWO CITIES*

C. Baldridge, "Alternatives to Bourgeois Individualism in *A Tale of Two Cities*," *Studies in English Literature, 1500–1900*, vol. 30, Autumn 1990.

Charles E. Beckwith, ed., *Twentieth-Century Interpretations of* A Tale of Two Cites: *A Collection of Critical Essays.* Englewood Cliffs, NJ: Prentice-Hall, 1972.

Harold Bloom, ed., *Charles Dickens'* A Tale of Two Cities: *Modern Critical Interpretations.* New York: Chelsea House, 1987.

Franklin E. Court, "Boots, Barbarism, and the New Order in Dickens' *A Tale of Two Cities,*" *Victorians Institute Journal,* vol. 9, 1980–1981.

Richard J. Dunn, "A Tale of Two Dramatists," *Dickens Studies Annual,* vol. 12, 1983.

Edward M. Eigner, "Charles Darnay and Revolutionary Identity," *Dickens Studies Annual,* vol. 12, 1983.

Elliot L. Gilbert, "'To Awake from History': Carlyle, Thackeray and *A Tale of Two Cities,*" *Dickens Studies Annual,* vol. 12. 1983.

J.F. Hamilton, "Terrorizing the Feminine in Hugo, Dickens, and France," *Symposium,* vol. 48, Fall 1994.

Henry I. Hubert, *Charles Dickens'* A Tale of Two Cities. New York: Simon and Schuster, 1964.

Albert D. Hutter, "Nation and Generation in *A Tale of Two Cities,*" *PMLA,* vol. 93, no. 3, May 1978.

Edgar Johnson, Introduction to Charles Dickens, *A Tale of Two Cities.* New York: Washington Square Press, 1960.

John Kucich, "The Purity of Violence: *A Tale of Two Cities,*" *Dickens Studies Annual,* vol. 8, 1980.

Carol Mackay, "The Rhetoric of Soliloquy in *The French Revolution* and *A Tale of Two Cities,*" *Dickens Studies Annual,* vol. 12, 1983.

Leonard Manheim, "A Tale of Two Characters: A Study in Multiple Projection," *Dickens Studies Annual,* vol. 1, 1970.

David D. Marcus, "The Carylean Vision of *A Tale of Two Cities,*" *Studies in the Novel,* vol. 8, no. 1, Spring 1976.

J.M. Rignall, "Dickens and the Catastrophic Continuum of History in *A Tale of Two Cities,*" *ELH,* vol. 51, no. 3, Fall 1984.

L. Robson, "The Angels in Dickens' House—Women in *A Tale of Two Cities,*" *Dalhousie Review,* vol. 72, Fall 1992.

Andrew Sanders, *The Companion to* A Tale of Two Cities. London: Unwin Hyman, 1988.

WORKS BY CHARLES DICKENS

Sketches by Boz, The Village Coquettes, The Strange Gentleman (1836)

The Pickwick Papers, Is She His Wife? (1837)

Oliver Twist, Sketches of Young Gentlemen (1838)

Nicholas Nickleby (1839)

Sketches of Young Couples (1840)

Barnaby Rudge, The Old Curiosity Shop (1841)

American Notes (1842)

A Christmas Carol (1843)

The Chimes, Martin Chuzzlewit (1844)

The Battle of Life: A Love Story, Pictures from Italy, The Cricket on the Hearth (1846)

Dombey and Son, The Haunted Man (1848)

David Copperfield (1850)

Mr. Nightingale's Diary (1851)

A Child's History of England (1852)

Bleak House (1853)

Hard Times (1854)

Little Dorrit (1855)

A Tale of Two Cities (1859)

Great Expectations, The Uncommercial Traveler (1861)

Our Mutual Friend (1864)

No Thoroughfare (1867)

George Silverman's Explanation (1868)

The Mystery of Edwin Drood (unfinished) (1870)

INDEX